*Dedicated to the students at Dunlavy, Holbrook, Northside,
and Pine Street Elementary Schools.*

Thanks for your help in realizing our dream.

Linking Picture Books to Standards

Written and Illustrated by
Brenda S. Copeland and Patricia A. Messner

LIBRARIES
UNLIMITED
A Member of the Greenwood Publishing Group

Westport, Connecticut • London

Library of Congress Cataloging-in-Publication Data

Copeland, Brenda S.
   Linking picture books to standards / written and illustrated by Brenda S. Copeland
and Patricia A. Messner.
      p. cm.
   Includes bibliographical references and index.
   ISBN 1–59158–088–9 (alk. paper)
   1. Picture books for children—Educational aspects—United States. 2. Language
arts—Standards—United States. 3. Elementary school libraries—Activity programs—
United States. 4. Children—Books and reading—United States. I. Messner, Patricia A.
II. Title.
LB1044.9.P49C66   2003

   372.133'5—dc22   2003053876

British Library Cataloguing in Publication Data is available.

Library of Congress Catalog Card Number: 2003053876
ISBN: 1–59158–088–9

First published in 2003

Libraries Unlimited, 88 Post Road West, Westport, CT 06881
A Member of the Greenwood Publishing Group, Inc.
www.lu.com

Printed in the United States of America

The paper used in this book complies with the
Permanent Paper Standard issued by the National
Information Standards Organization (Z39.48-1984).

10 9 8 7 6 5 4 3 2 1

Contents

Preface · vii

Standards for the English Language Arts · ix

Part 1: Retelling Favorites

1 *The Big Green Pocketbook* 3
2 *The Napping House* 6
3 *Joseph Had a Little Overcoat* 9
4 *Welcome Back to Pokeweed Public School* 13
5 *Rabbit Food* 16
6 *The Teeny Tiny Teacher* 19
7 *The Jacket I Wear in the Snow* 23
8 *Alligator Baby* 26
9 *If You Take a Mouse to the Movies* 29
10 *Is Your Mama a Llama?* 34

Part 2: Comprehension Favorites

11 *The Frog Principal* 41
12 *Maxwell's Magic Mix-Up* 46
13 *Franklin's Halloween* 50
14 *Cobweb Christmas* 53
15 *Mrs. Piccolo's Easy Chair* 57
16 *D.W. the Picky Eater* 60
17 *The Bag I'm Taking to Grandma's* 63
18 *Strega Nona Takes a Vacation* 66
19 *The Rainbow Fish* 69
20 *Timothy Goes to School* 73

Part 3: Story Elements Favorites

21 *Bark, George* 79
22 *Big Al* 82
23 *Cindy Ellen: A Wild Western Cinderella* 86
24 *The Lady with the Alligator Purse* 89
25 *Grandpa's Teeth* 96
26 *The Little Red Hen (Makes a Pizza)* 100
27 *Miss Spider's Tea Party* 103
28 *'Twas the Night Before Thanksgiving* 107
29 *When Winter Comes* 115
30 *Show and Tell Bunnies* 117

Part 4: Author Favorites

31 Eric Carle Study: *The Grouchy Ladybug* and *The Very Hungry Caterpillar* 127
32 David Shannon Study: *David Goes to School* 137
33 Jan Brett Study: *The Mitten* and *The Hat* 142
34 Louise Borden Study: *A. Lincoln and Me* 150
35 Mike Thaler Study: *The Librarian from the Black Lagoon* 155

Appendix · 159
Web Resources · 163
Bibliography · 165
Index · 167

Preface

We hope you enjoy our collection of storybook favorites. The lessons have been tested in our library classrooms and are aligned with the national language arts standards from the National Council of Teachers of English. They can be found at www.ncte.org and also in *Standards for the English Language Arts* (sponsored by NCTE and IRA, Urbana, IL: NCTE, 1996). Questions for the comprehension section of this book have been designed using Benjamin Bloom's *Taxonomy of Educational Objectives: Handbook I, The Cognitive Domain* (New York: David McKay, 1956). We designed these lessons for 30 to 45 minutes of library time.

There are four sections in this book: retelling, comprehension, elements of a story, and author studies. The lessons may be used in a regular classroom or library. Each lesson lists the applicable language arts national standards and provides objectives, skills, props, and materials needed.

Keep the following helpful hints in mind as you examine our lesson plans. Trips to a local thrift store or garage sales can result in a gold mine of costumes, props, and extra books for your story time. Keep a list of needed items with you when you go out. This will help remind you of the story characters and necessary props. We have included ideas for costumes in several of the lessons, which the teacher or librarian can wear. Make your costumes simple and easy to change. Use sizes that are big enough to slip over your school clothes. Better yet, use items such as vest, hats, and jackets that add to whatever you are wearing for the day. Plan your day's wardrobe accordingly.

Store props and costumes in plastic bins. Tape a list inside that indicates when and where you used the story or unit last. Always keep an extra copy of the book with the unit or story props. Your library copies will then be available for eager students.

High school clubs can help out elementary classes by taping stories, designing props, and making puppets. This will give your students a chance to hear other readers, and both age groups will reap huge benefits. Leave the books and story props out for centers in your classrooms or library and watch the magic happen. Smiles will abound, and the extra effort will make these stories lifetime favorites that will be read over and over again.

Standards for the English Language Arts*

NL-ENG.K12.1 READING FOR PERSPECTIVE

Students read a wide range of print and nonprint texts to build an understanding of texts, of themselves, and of the culture of the United States and the world; to acquire new information; to respond to the needs and the demands of society and the workplace; and for personal fulfillment. Among these texts are fiction and nonfiction, classic and contemporary works.

NL-ENG.K12.2 UNDERSTANDING THE HUMAN EXPERIENCE

Students read a wide range of literature from many periods in many genres to build an understanding of many dimensions of human experience.

NL-ENG.K12.3 EVALUATION STRATEGIES

Students apply a wide range of strategies to comprehend, interpret, evaluate, and appreciate texts. They draw on their prior experience, their interactions with other readers and writers, their knowledge of word meaning and of other texts, their word identification strategies, and their understanding of textual features (e.g., sound-letter correspondence, sentence structure, context, graphics).

NL-ENG.K-12.4 COMMUNICATION SKILLS

Students adjust their use of spoken, written, and visual language (e.g., conventions, style, vocabulary) to communicate effectively with a variety of audiences and for different purposes.

NL-ENG.K-12.5 COMMUNICATION STRATEGIES

Students employ a wide range of strategies as they write and use different writing process elements appropriately to communicate with different audiences for a variety of purposes.

NL-ENG.K12.7 EVALUATING DATA

Students conduct research on issues and interest by generating ideas and questions, and by posing problems. They gather, evaluate, and synthesize data from a variety of sources (e.g., print and nonprint texts, artifacts, people) to communicate their discoveries in ways that suit their purpose and audience.

NL-ENG.K-12.8 DEVELOPING RESEARCH SKILLS

Students use a variety of technological and information resources (e.g., libraries, databases, computer networks, video) to gather and synthesize information and to create and communicate knowledge.

---

*Standards for the English Language Arts, by the International Reading Association and the National Council of Teachers of English, Copyright 1996 by the International Reading Association and the National Council of Teachers of English. Reprinted with permission.

NL-ENG.K-12.11 PARTICIPATING IN SOCIETY

Students participate as knowledgeable, reflective, creative, and critical members of a variety of literacy communities.

NL-ENG.K-12.12 APPLYING LANGUAGE SKILLS

Students use spoken, written, and visual language to accomplish their own purpose (e.g., for learning, enjoyment, persuasion, and the exchange of information).

Part 1

Retelling Favorites

1
The Big Green Pocketbook

By Candice Ransom

From Candice Ransom. *The Big Green Pocketbook.* New York, HarperCollins, 1993.

Language Arts National Standards

NL-ENG.K-12.4 Communication Skills

Students adjust their use of spoken, written, and visual language (e.g., conventions, style, vocabulary) to communicate effectively with a variety of audiences and for different purposes.

NL-ENG.K-12.5 Communication Strategies

Students employ a wide range of strategies as they write and use different writing process elements appropriately to communicate with different audiences for a variety of purposes.

Skills	Retelling in chronological order Creative writing

Objective

Students will be able to place the store signs in the proper sequence as they recall the events in the story.

Grade Level	Second grade

Props	Green pocketbook Key chain Box of new crayons Two suckers, one yellow and one purple Two tickets Paper with "Sally Ann" typed in both uppercase and lowercase letters Pocket calendar (with a new cover with the name Puffin Cleaners on it)

Materials	Poster board for store signs Newspaper advertisements

Instructions

Make store signs with the name of each place Sally Ann and her mother visited on their shopping day.

Places

Jewelry store

Insurance office

Bank

Puffin Cleaners

Drug store

Two bus stops (trip to town and trip home)

5-and-10 store

Make store signs, with the name of the business in large letters. Decorate the signs using newspaper advertisements that the students will recognize or paper cutouts. *Example:* The insurance office can have an umbrella cut out of paper or fabric.

Lesson

Step 1: Read the story to students.

Step 2: Mix up the store signs and see whether students can remember the stops that Sally and her mother made. Make a street of shops on the floor, lining them up train fashion, starting with the bus stop. Make a second bus stop sign to denote getting on the bus for the return trip.

Step 3: Place the items from the stores inside the pocketbook. Choose children to come up and pull out each item from the pocketbook. Students can match each item with the store it came from.

Step 4: **Worksheet:** Write another adventure for the green pocketbook. Brainstorm some ideas. Where will Sally and her pocketbook go next? As the students write their stories, stress that they need to include the items that they collect in the new stores.

Closure

Have students share their stories.

Teacher's Notes:

The Big Green Pocketbook
by Candice Ransom

Write another shopping adventure.
Pretend that school is starting and Mary
Ann and her mother are looking for new
school clothes. What will Mary Ann find
to place inside the pocketbook?

2
The Napping House

By Audrey Wood

From Audrey Wood. *The Napping House.* San Diego: Harcourt Brace Jovanovich, 1984.

Language Arts National Standards

NL-ENG.K12.1 Reading for Perspective

Students read a wide range of print and nonprint texts to build an understanding of texts, of themselves, and of the culture of the United States and the world; to acquire new information; to respond to the needs and the demands of society and the workplace; and for personal fulfillment. Among these texts are fiction and nonfiction, classic and contemporary works.

NL-ENG.K12.3 Evaluation Strategies

Students apply a wide range of strategies to comprehend, interpret, evaluate, and appreciate texts. They draw on their prior experience, their interactions with other readers and writers, their knowledge of word meaning and of other texts, their word identification strategies, and their understanding of textual features (e.g., sound-letter correspondence, sentence structure, context, graphics).

Skills	Retelling
	Sequencing

Objective

The students will be able to retell the events of the story by using the stuffed animals and be able to put them in proper order as they appear in the story.

Grade Level	Second grade
Costume	Granny nightgown
	Slippers
	Nightcap (shower or curler cap)
Props	Granny doll
	Boy doll
	Girl doll
	Dog
	Cat
	Mouse
	Flea (two two-inch hearts cut out of paper, glued and squashed together at the point)
	Blanket

Materials   Shoe box
Scrap fabric and lace

Instructions: Prepare the Box

Turn the box upside down and hot glue fabric onto the box so that the box is completely covered. Start with the flat top first and then cut edges so that it folds in like an envelope. Around the side of the box glue eyelet or gathered lace. Use lace that is wide enough so that the effect is a dust ruffle. This will make the box look something like a doll bed. Add a pillow by cutting, sewing, and stuffing a small piece of fabric to match.

Lesson

Step 1: Spread a blanket or quilt on the floor and invite the students to sit on the blanket or quilt as the story is read.

Step 2: On the second reading, ask the students to be the characters. Assign parts and let students pretend to go to sleep at their part of the story. Make sure to pick someone to be the flea that wakes everyone up.

Step 3: Have the students retell the story using the shoebox bed and characters. Use the question "What happened next in the story?"

Closure

Follow up with the crossword puzzle worksheet.

Teacher's Notes:

The Napping House
by Audrey Wood
Worksheet

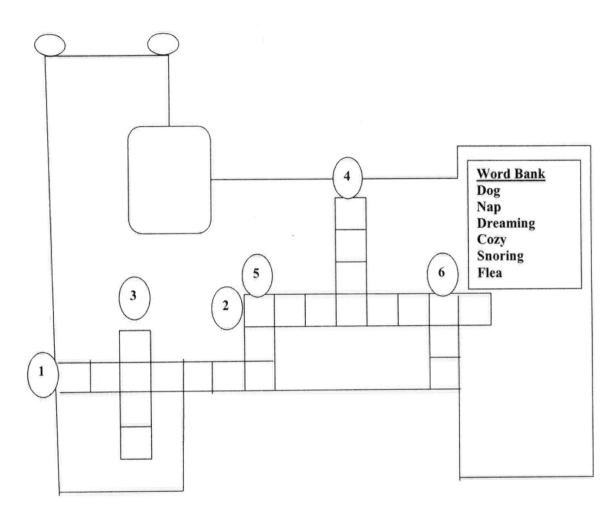

Word Bank
Dog
Nap
Dreaming
Cozy
Snoring
Flea

Questions:

1. Granny is _____.
2. The child is _____.
3. The bed is _____.
4. Who does not go to sleep? _____
5. Who is dozing? _____
6. Almost everyone is taking a _____.

3
Joseph Had a Little Overcoat

By Simms Taback

Taback, Simms. *Joseph Had a Little Overcoat.* New York: Viking Press, 1999.

Language Arts National Standards

NL-ENG.K12.1 Reading for Perspective

Students read a wide range of print and nonprint texts to build an understanding of texts, of themselves, and of the cultures of the United States and the world; to acquire new information; to respond to the needs and demands of society and the workplace; and for personal fulfillment. Among these texts are fiction and nonfiction, classic and contemporary works.

NL-ENG.K12.3 Evaluation Strategies

Students apply a wide range of strategies to comprehend, interpret, evaluate, and appreciate texts. They draw on their prior experience, their interactions with other readers and writers, their knowledge of word meaning and of other texts, their word identification strategies, and their understanding of textual features (e.g., sound-letter correspondence, sentence structure, context graphics).

Skills	Story sequencing Main character

Objective

Students will be able to place the clothing on the doll in the correct order as the items appear in the story.

Grade Level	First and second grades
Costume	Oversized man's overcoat and hat
Materials	Craft paint (flesh, white, and black) Package of curly craft hair Wool material for overcoat Scrap fabric for pants and shirt Velcro Wire for glasses Heavy cardboard or thin wood

9

Instructions: Patterns

Using the worksheet pattern, cut Joseph out of heavy cardboard or thin wood. Enlarge the Joseph and clothing patterns to the size that you wish to make. Paint the face, hands, and boots. Cut out a shirt and paints from fabric and glue them onto the Joseph cutout. They do not need to be removed. Glue curly craft hair onto Joseph and use a thin piece of wire to fashion a pair of glasses. Glue the glasses into place so students won't play with them.

Tip: Don't buy new fabric—cut up an old wool skirt or man's suit coat. You can find a wool item at a garage sale or thrift store. Something with a close weave that will not fray at the edges is your best choice. Use Velcro to attach the pieces onto the next garment. Each one should be hidden from view like the story pictures.

Lesson

Step 1: Greet students wearing the oversized overcoat and hat.

Step 2: Introduce the story and talk about the Caldecott Award. Explain that this story was chosen because it was the best picture book for the year.

Step 3: Read the story as written

Step 4: Review the sequence of the story by removing each article of clothing from the Joseph cutout. Students will enjoy guessing. Layer items so they are covered by the top piece. If students have trouble, review the pages again.

Closure

Copy Joseph the doll onto tagboard for each student. Copy the clothes onto regular copy paper for each student. Have students cut out Joseph and the clothes. Using scrap paper, students will cut out the scarf, button, and tie. Students will color and decorate Joseph. Students will take turns retelling the story to each other using their paper dolls.

Teacher's Notes:

Joseph Had a Little Overcoat
by Simms Taback
Patterns

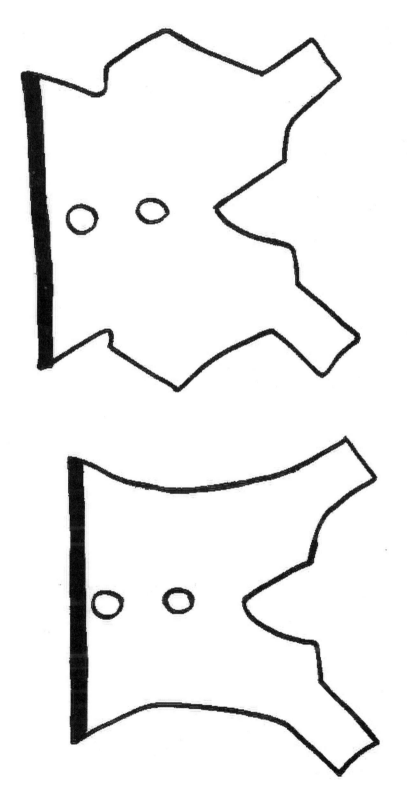

Joseph Had a Little Overcoat
by Simms Taback
Patterns

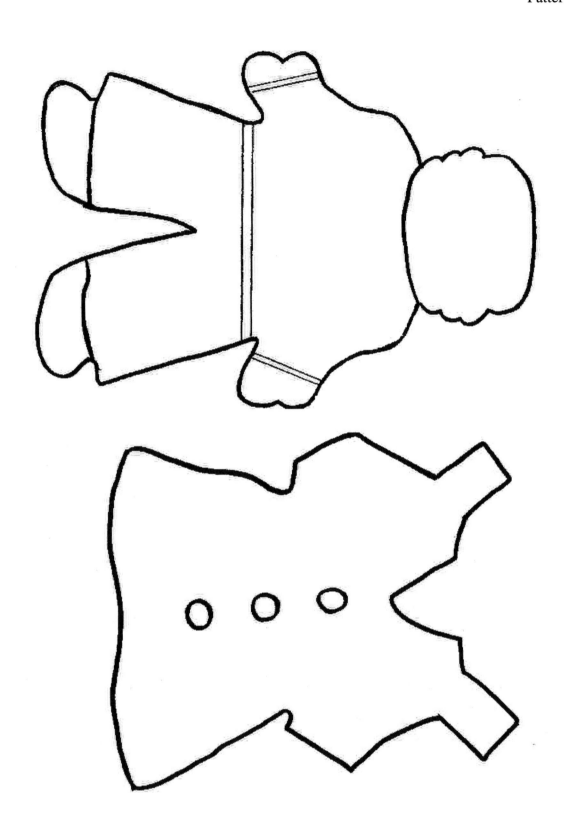

4

Welcome Back to Pokeweed Public School

By John Bianchi

From John Bianchi. *Welcome Back to Pokeweed Public School*. Buffalo, N.Y.: Bungalo Books, 1996.

Language Arts National Standards

NL-ENG.K-12.3 Evaluation Strategies

Students apply a wide range of strategies to comprehend, interpret, evaluate, and appreciate texts. They draw on their prior experience, their interactions with other readers and writers, their knowledge of word meaning and of other texts, their word identification strategies, and their understanding of textual features (e.g., sound-letter correspondence, sentence structure, context, graphics).

Skills
Story sequencing
Reading comprehension

Objective

The students will be able to place the picture cards in the correct order as they appear in the story and also be able to answer the comprehension questions.

Grade Level
Kindergarten through second grade

Materials
Craft paint
Cardboard
Utility knife
Heavy paper for pockets or library card pocket
Pictures

Instructions

Using 3-by-5-inch index cards, cut out pictures from magazines. Cut small cards so that they fit inside the card pockets, and laminate them for longer wear.

Picture Cards
Bus ride to Pokeweed School
Ms. Mudwortz's classroom
Opening-day ceremony
Computer lab
Walking field trip
Big Scoop Ice Cream Factory
Bus ride home

Cardboard School

Cut the cardboard to look like the worksheet. Fold the cardboard with the card pockets inside. It should close so it looks like the front of the building with the pockets hidden inside. Paint and decorate the outside to look as much like the book jacket as possible.

Comprehension Questions

Who paid for the ice cream treat?

How did he pay?

Why did the students go for a walk?

What did the students see on their field trip?

Why did the school flood?

Who cleaned up the mess? What was her name?

Lesson

Step 1: Read the story aloud.

Step 2: Place the cards out on the table so that all students can see. Discuss each picture and have students point out the parts of the story that they represent. Have students select each card and place it in the correct order on the inside of the cardboard school.

Step 3: Use the comprehension questions to review the students' understanding of the story.

Closure

Worksheet for follow-up activity: Use the worksheet to create a sequel to this story. What happened next at the school? Students can cut out pictures or draw their own Pokeweed School.

Kindergarten: Draw and color a picture for the second day of school at Pokeweed.

First and second grades: Write or cut out pictures for the second day of school at Pokeweed.

Teacher's Notes:

Welcome Back to Pokeweed Public School
by John Bianchi
Pattern

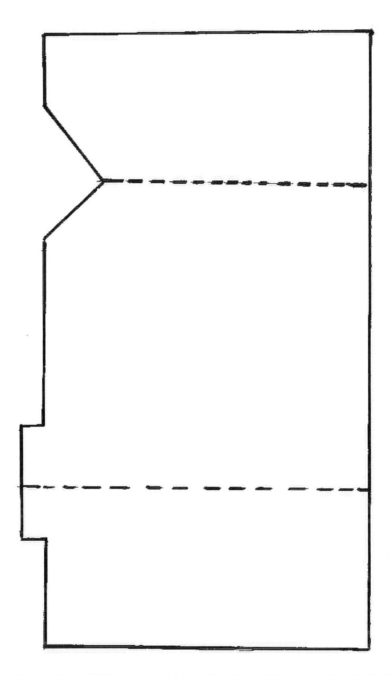

1. Cut on the solid lines and fold on the dotted lines to make the Pokeweed
    School.

2. Cut out pictures from magazines to show what happened at Pokeweed
    School on the second day of class.

3. Glue your pictures inside the school and share the story with a friend.

5
Rabbit Food

By Susanna Gretz

From Susanna Gretz. *Rabbit Food*. Cambridge, Mass.: Candlewick Press, 1999.

Language Arts National Standards

NL-ENG.K-12.3 Evaluation Strategies

Students apply a wide range of strategies to comprehend, interpret, evaluate, and appreciate texts. They draw on their prior experience, their interactions with other readers and writers, their knowledge of word meaning and of other texts, their word identification strategies, and their understanding of textual features (e.g., sound-letter correspondence, sentence structure, context, graphics).

Skills   Retelling

Objective

The students will be able to use the finger puppets to retell the story.

Grade Level   Kindergarten

Costume   Apron with pockets (from craft stores)

Materials   Felt in several spring colors
                    Cotton balls
                    Movable eyes
                    Hot glue and glue gun
                    Tube paints

Instructions

Stencil or decorate the apron with fabric paint. Make lots of finger puppet rabbits using the worksheet pattern. Number each puppet on the back with a marker. Make enough so that each student can have a puppet during the activity. Keep them hidden in the pockets of the apron until after the story has been read.

Lesson

Step 1: Read the story aloud.

Step 2: Give out finger puppets. Give students time to play with them. They can even take them to the shelves and let the puppets help choose a book. Tell students that today the rabbits will help them find rabbit books to check out. Once students have selected their books, they may read to their puppets.

Step 3: Move back to the circle again and have students stand and tell what happened in the story, using their puppets. Use the number system. Call out numbers until all the students have had a turn. Students can place their puppets inside the pockets of the apron as they finish.

Teacher's Notes:

Rabbit Food
by Susanna Gretz
Pattern

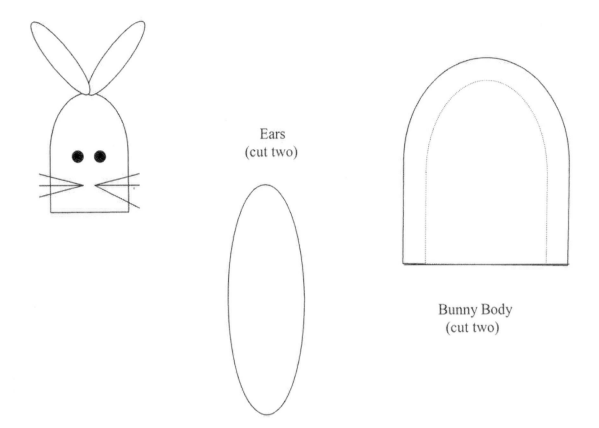

Ears
(cut two)

Bunny Body
(cut two)

1. Cut several rabbits out of felt.

2. Glue the bodies of the bunnies together on the dotted lines, leaving the bottoms open to slide over the fingers.

3. Attach the ears so they stick up.

4. Glue cotton balls to the backs and movable eyes to the fronts.

5. Use tube paint for the noses and whiskers.

6
The Teeny Tiny Teacher

By Stephanie Calmenson

From Stephanie Calmenson. *The Teeny Tiny Teacher.* New York: Scholastic Press, 1998.

Language Arts National Standards

NL-ENG.K-12.4 Communication Skills

Students adjust their use of spoken, written, and visual language (e.g., conventions, style, vocabulary} to communicate effectively with a variety of audiences and for different purposes.

NL-ENG.K-12.5 Communication Strategies

Students employ a wide range of strategies as they write and use different writing process elements appropriately to communicate with different audiences for a variety of purposes.

NL-ENG.K-12.3 Evaluation Strategies

Students apply a wide range of strategies to comprehend, interpret, evaluate, and appreciate texts. They draw on their prior experience, their interactions with other readers and writers, their knowledge of word meaning and of other texts, their word identification strategies, and their understanding of textual features (e.g., sound-letter correspondence, sentence structure, context, graphics).

NL-ENG.K-12.11 Participating in Society

Students participate as knowledgeable, reflective, creative, and critical members of a variety of literacy communities.

Skills
Shared writing
Writing and illustrating a class book
Retelling

Objective
Students will be able to retell the story and create another story using the same format.

Grade Level   Second grade

Materials   Blue construction paper
Shoebox
8 ½-by-11-inch red spiral notebook
A penny
Large pink eraser
Artificial flowers

> Dominoes
> Dice
> Buttons
> Matchsticks
> Small notebook
> Small dolls (to represent teacher and students)
> Facial tissue

Instructions

Cover a shoebox with blue construction paper and use the red spiral notebook for the roof. Place a penny over the outside of the door. Use four sharp yellow pencils for the corners of the schoolhouse. Us a large pink eraser for the front step and place flowers around the outside of the shoebox. Decorate the outside with windows and a door. Add dominoes, dice, buttons, match sticks for table legs, and a small notebook to make the inside of the box look like the school in the story. Small dolls will be needed for the teacher and students. Also make a ghost out of a facial tissue.

Lesson

Step 1: Introduce the book by looking at the cover and asking questions: "What do you think this book will be about? What do *teeny* and *tiny* mean? Have you heard a story like this before?" Share some items that would show the difference between small and tiny, tiny and big. Write up word cards or put words on the board so that students can see them. Share the story *The Three Bears.* This story has many examples of small, tiny, and big.

Step 2: Tell the story using the schoolhouse and contents that you made.

Step 3: Worksheet: Use the fun dot-to-dot sheet.

Follow-up Lesson

Step1: Review the story by alternating between reading a page and letting a student tell what happened. Talk about the teeny tiny things in the story. Brainstorm ideas for a class book. *Examples:* The Teeny Tiny Librarian, Music Teacher, Gym Teacher, etc. Write some ideas on the board. After picking one for the class to write about, do a story web before starting the class story.

Step 2: Record the story on large paper, one sentence to each page. Pair up students to illustrate the pages. Share the completed pages and have students reorganize them in the correct order. Some students can make the title page for the book. Bind the book and circulate it as a regular book.

Closure

Share the bound book with the class.

Teacher's Notes:

The Teeny Tiny Teacher
by Stephanie Calmenson
Story Web

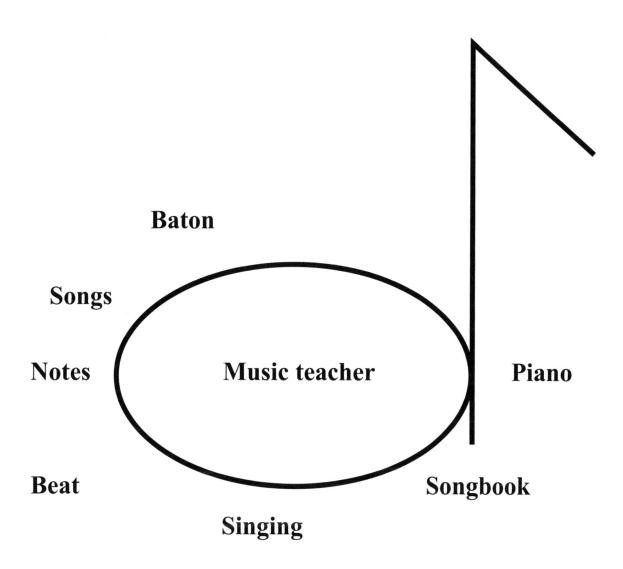

Baton

Songs

Notes   **Music teacher**   **Piano**

Beat

Singing   **Songbook**

The Teeny Tiny Teacher
by Stephanie Calmenson
Worksheet

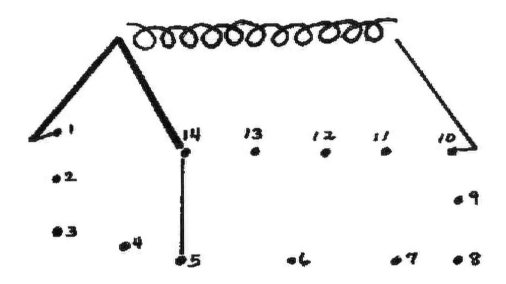

Complete the dot-to-dot, add windows and a door, and make
it look like the Teeny Tiny School.

7

The Jacket I Wear in the Snow

By Shirley Neitzel

From Shirley Neitzel. *The Jacket I Wear in the Snow*. New York: Greenwillow Books, 1989.

Language Arts National Standards

NL-ENG.K12.1 Reading for Perspective

Students read a wide range of print and nonprint texts to build an understanding of texts, of themselves, and of the cultures of the United States and the world; to acquire new information; to respond to the needs and demands of society and the workplace; and for personal fulfillment. Among these texts are fiction and nonfiction, classic and contemporary works.

NL-ENG.K12.2 Understanding the Human Experience

Students read a wide range of literature from many periods in many genres to build an understanding of many dimensions of human experience.

NL-ENG.K-12.3 Evaluation Strategies

Students apply a wide range of strategies to comprehend, interpret, evaluate, and appreciate texts. They draw on their prior experience, their interactions with other readers and writers, their knowledge of word meaning and of other texts, their word identification strategies, and their understanding of textual features (e.g., sound-letter correspondence, sentence structure, context, graphics).

NL-ENG.K-12.11 Participating in Society

Students participate as knowledgeable, reflective, creative, and critical members of a variety of literacy communities.

Skills   Retelling
Creative writing

Objective

Students will be able to retell the story using the phrases from the story. Students will also write a revised story and arrange the clothes in the proper order as they occur in the text.

Grade Level   Second grade

Costume   Winter hat, scarf, and mittens

Materials

Sentence strips
Markers
Construction paper or wall paper for the paper clothes
Clothes line and pins
Story parts written on sentence strips

Instructions

Make appropriate clothes, jacket, scarf, hat, gloves, sweater, jeans, and long underwear from paper.

Lesson

Step 1: Greet the students wearing a hat, mittens, and a scarf. Explain that this story is about what we would wear when headed outside to play in the cold weather. Read the story aloud.

Step 2: Hang the paper clothes on a clothesline that is strung between two chairs in the classroom. Ask the students, "Are they in the correct order? Would we put the clothes on in the same order if we were going out in the snow?" Allow for some share time and let kids discover that things are put on wrong in the story. They should pick up on this without any help. Put the clothes on the line first as they appear in the story and then again as the students would put them on to go out in the snow.

Step 3: Pass out the sentence strips. Read the story again and have students come to the front as their phrases are read.

Step 4: Students will rewrite the story using the worksheet.

Closure

Share stories in a circle as time allows.

Teacher's Notes:

The Clothes I Wear in the Snow

By _____

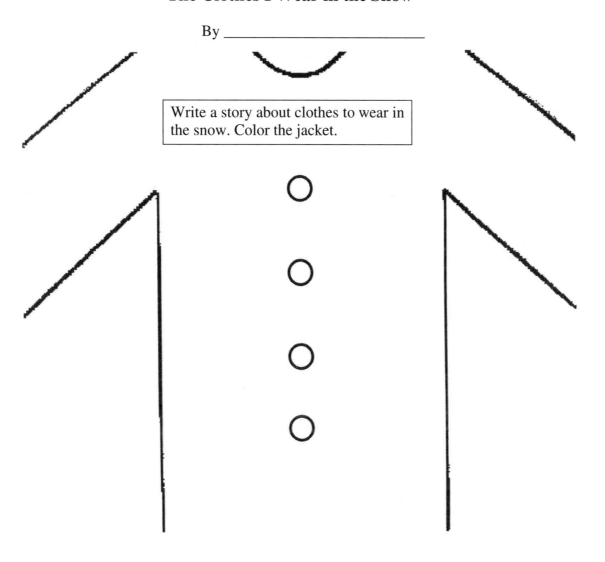

Write a story about clothes to wear in the snow. Color the jacket.

8

Alligator Baby

By Robert Munsch

From Robert Munsch. *Alligator Baby*. New York: Scholastic, 1997.

Language Arts National Standards

NL-ENG.K12.1 Reading for Perspective

Students read a wide range of print and nonprint texts to build an understanding of texts, of themselves, and of the cultures of the United States and the world; to acquire new information; to respond to the needs and demands of society and the workplace; and for personal fulfillment. Among these texts are fiction and nonfiction, classic and contemporary works.

NL-ENG.K12.2 Understanding the Human Experience

Students read a wide range of literature from many periods in many genres to build an understanding of many dimensions of human experience.

NL-ENG.K-12.3 Evaluation Strategies

Students apply a wide range of strategies to comprehend, interpret, evaluate, and appreciate texts. They draw on their prior experience, their interactions with other readers and writers, their knowledge of word meaning and of other texts, their word identification strategies, and their understanding of textual features (e.g., sound-letter correspondence, sentence structure, context, graphics).

NL-ENG.K-12.11 Participating in Society

Students participate as knowledgeable, reflective, creative, and critical members of a variety of literacy communities.

Skills	Retelling Oral communication

Objective

Students will be able to retell the story using the phrases from the story. Students will also write a revised story and arrange the clothes in the proper order.

Grade Level	First and second grades
Props	Baby doll and blanket Stuffed alligator, seal, and small gorilla Baby blanket Diaper bag for storage of materials

Materials   Poster board or construction paper for repetitive phases.

Repetitive phrases

Blam, blam, blam, blam, blam

Kristen, would you like to see your baby brother?

Now, Kristen, don't be jealous.

Aaaaaahhhhhaaaaa!

Goodness, we've got the wrong baby!

Instructions

Write or type repetitive phrases on paper and laminate them.

Lesson

Step 1: Read the story aloud. Make sure that the props are all hidden in the diaper bag.

Step 2: Talk about what phrases are repetitive.

Step 3: Assign students repetitive parts and then retell the story using the props. Students will respond in the appropriate places.

Closure

Students will complete the worksheet, matching the characters in the story with the correct phrases.

Teacher's Notes:

Alligator Baby
by Robert Munsch
Worksheet

Draw a line from the character to the right words.
Color the baby bottle

Kristen   Varooooooooooommmmm

Kristen's Mother   Waaa, waaa, waaa, waaa.

Car   Now, Kristen, don't be jealous!

Baby Alligator   Bathtub

Baby Seal   Chandelier

Baby Gorilla   Fish Tank

Kristen's Baby Brother   That is not my baby brother!

9
If You Take a Mouse to the Movies

By Laura Numeroff

From Laura Numeroff. *If You Take a Mouse to the Movies.* New York: HarperCollins, 2000.

Language Arts National Standards

NL-ENG.K-12.4 Communication Skills

Students adjust their use of spoken, written, and visual language (e.g., conventions, style, vocabulary) to communicate effectively with a variety of audiences and for different purposes.

NL-ENG.K-12.5 Communication Strategies

Students employ a wide range of strategies as they write and use different writing process elements appropriately to communicate with different audiences for a variety of purposes.

Skills	Retelling Sequencing

Objective

Students will be able to retell the story in proper sequence using the flannel objects.

Grade Level	First and second grades
Props	Small stuffed mouse
Materials	Felt (white, purple, tan, and green)(See pattern for shapes.) Flannel board Puffy paint (for details on shapes)

Instructions

Cut shapes from the felt and decorate them with the puffy paint.

Lesson

Step 1: Give the students clues. See if they can guess the title of the book that you plan to read. Place the book, along with the mouse and the clues written on cards, in a brown paper bag.

- Clue one: Mouse is the main character
- Clue two: Title starts out (If You Take). Write this on a card and make it look like a movie ticket.
- Clue three: It is Christmas time in this story. Write this on a piece of green paper that has been cut in the shape of a Christmas tree.

Step 2: Show the front of the book. Review the title and author. Show students where other books by the same author are located in the library.

Step 3: Read the story aloud.

Step 4: Lay out all flannel pieces so the students can see them. Explain that the students need to look for an object that would represent the first event in the story. Continue in this fashion until all the pieces have been placed in the correct order. Use the book to check the order of events.

Closure

Worksheet on sequencing: Put the correct words from the word bank unto the numbered spaces on the wall.

Teacher's Notes:

If You Take a Mouse to the Movies

By Laura Numeroff

Put the words in order to retell what happened in this story.

1.	**2.**	**3.**
4.		**5.**
6.	**7.**	

Word Bank

• blanket	• Christmas tree	• ornaments	• popcorn
• radio	• snowman	• snowball fight	

On the back of this paper, draw your favorite snowball fight.

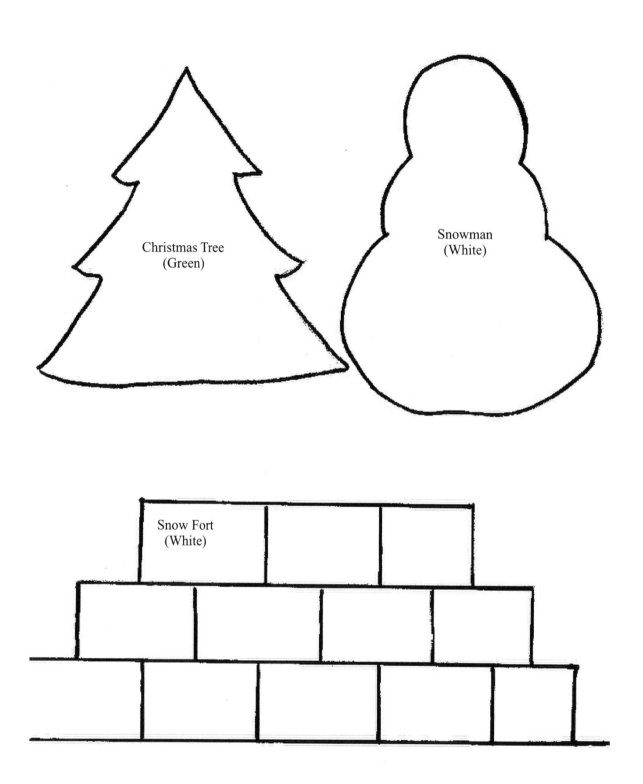

Christmas Tree
(Green)

Snowman
(White)

Snow Fort
(White)

If You Take a Mouse to the Movies
by Laura Numeroff
Pattern

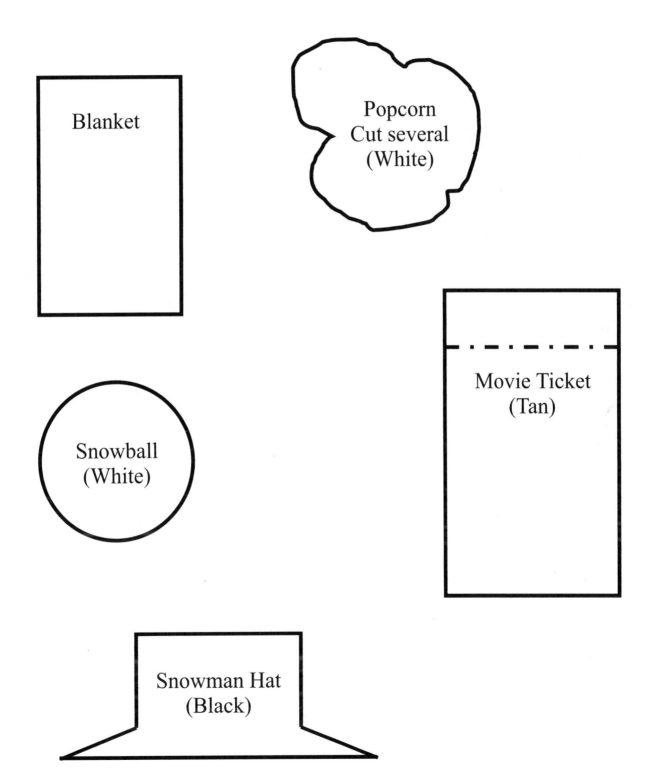

Blanket

Popcorn
Cut several
(White)

Snowball
(White)

Movie Ticket
(Tan)

Snowman Hat
(Black)

10
Is Your Mama a Llama?

By Deborah Guarino

From Deborah Guarino. *Is Your Mama a Llama?* New York: Scholastic, 1989.

Language Arts National Standards

NL-ENG.K-12.4 Communication Skills

Students adjust their use of spoken, written, and visual language (e.g., conventions, style, vocabulary) to communicate effectively with a variety of audiences and for different purposes.

NL-ENG.K-12.5 Communication Strategies

Students employ a wide range of strategies as they write and use different writing process elements appropriately to communicate with different audiences for a variety of purposes.

Skills Retelling

Objective

Students will be able to tell the beginning, middle, and end of the story.

Grade Level Second grade

Props Pictures or stuffed animals for the characters in the story: bat, swan, cow, seal, and kangaroo
Picture of your mother

Materials Two paper bags, lunch size

Instructions

Using the pattern worksheets, cut the face and two ears out of brown paper and attach them to paper bags to make the llamas. There are two llamas (Lloyd and Llyn). A stuffed animal or a puppet could be used. We have included the patterns as a backup since this animal might be harder to find.

Lesson

Step 1: Introduce the lesson by sharing the picture of your mother. Explain what things you do that are similar to what your mother does. Mention whether you both have the same hair color, etc. Introduce the title and author and point out that the little llama is looking for his mother. Ask the students to listen for things that help him find his mother. Does she look like him?

Step 2: Read the story aloud.

Step 3: Give out the characters, making sure to keep one of the llamas. Review the order of the animals in the story. Act out the story, letting the students tell the parts when their animals appear in the story. Review what the little llama found out at the end of the story.

Closure

Follow-up activity: Beginning, middle, and end worksheet.

Teacher's Notes:

Is Your Mama a Llama?
by Deborah Guarino
Worksheet

Write the beginning, middle, and end of the story.

Beginning

Lloyd, the llama,

_____

_____

_____

_____

_____

_____

Middle

Lloyd meets

_____

_____

_____

_____

_____

_____

End

Lloyd finds

_____

_____

_____

_____

_____

_____

Is Your Mama a Llama?
by Deborah Guarino
Pattern

Llama's ear

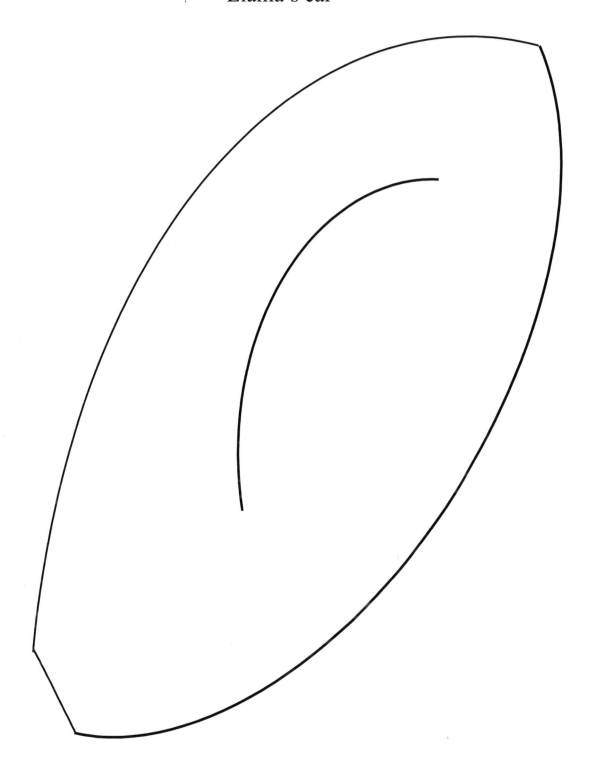

Is Your Mama a Llama?
by Deborah Guarino
Pattern

Llama's face

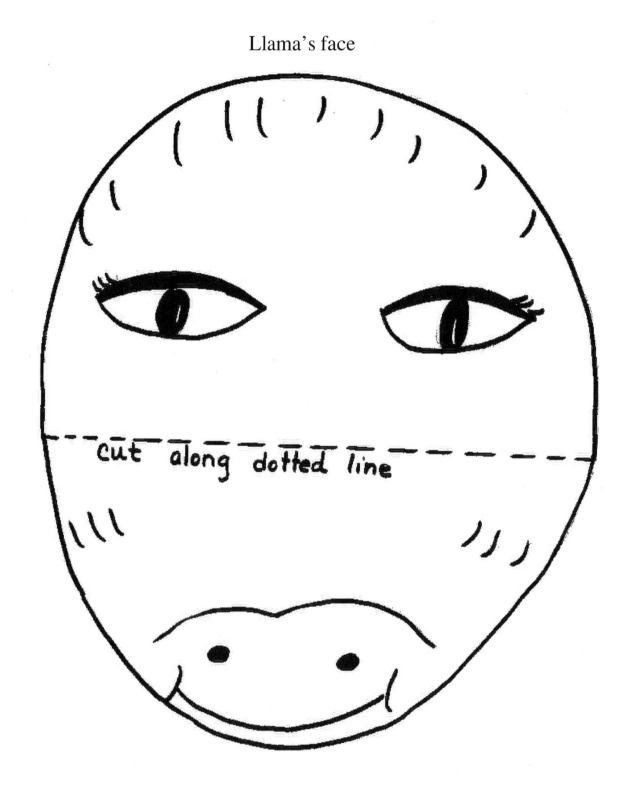

cut along dotted line

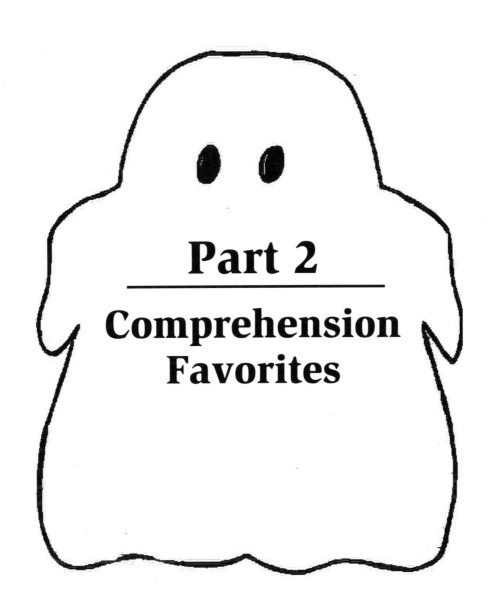

Part 2

Comprehension Favorites

11
The Frog Principal

By Stephanie Calmenson

From Stephanie Calmenson. *The Frog Principal.* New York: Scholastic Press, 2001.

Language Arts National Standards

NL-ENG.K-12.3 Evaluation Strategies

Students apply a wide range of strategies to comprehend, interpret, evaluate, and appreciate texts. They draw on their prior experience, their interactions with other readers and writes, their knowledge of word meaning and of other texts, their word identification strategies, and their understanding of textual features (e.g., sound-letter correspondence, sentence structure, context, graphics).

NL-ENG.K-12.4 Communication Skills

Students adjust their use of spoken, written, and visual language (e.g., conventions, style, and vocabulary) to communicate effectively with a variety of audiences and for different purposes.

NL-ENG.K-12.5 Communication Strategies

Students employ a wide range of strategies as they write and use different writing process elements appropriately to communicate with different audiences for a variety of purposes.

NL-ENG.K-12.12 Applying Language Skills

Students use spoken, written, and visual language to accomplish their own purposes (e.g., for learning, enjoyment, persuasion, and the exchange of information).

Skills   Reading comprehension
                Creative writing

Objective

The students will be able to answer the questions at the end of the story and then write a letter of thanks to their principal.

Grade Level   Kindergarten through second grade

Costumes   Man's suit coat
                Wacky looking tie

Props   Cardboard tie box covered with fancy paper

Small ties cut from construction paper (see pattern)

Enough ties so that each child in your class can wear one for the story

Materials   Construction paper

Questions typed or printed on small paper ties

Lesson

Step 1: Greet students dressed up in the suit coat and tie as Mr. Bundy, the main character in the story.

Step 2: Show the front cover of the book and let students predict what will happen to the principal in the story.

Step 3: Read the story and share the pictures with the class. If possible invite the principal to be a guest reader or make a tape with the principal reading the book. The students will be surprised to hear a mystery reader. This exercise is extra work, but it pays off.

Step 4: Pick students to come up and read the questions that have been placed in the tie box. Allow time to answer each question.

Step 5: Close out the story time by talking about the things a principal does. Ask students to share things they like about their principal.

Closure

Older students can write letters of thanks or appreciation to the principal (see worksheet). For younger classes, enlarge the pattern and make one large tie, then let kids write notes and draw little pictures. Write at the top of the tie: "I like my principal because: . . ."

Questions Labeled with Bloom's Levels of Thinking Taxonomy

Knowledge

1.   What did Mr. Bundy learn to eat by the end of the story?
2.   In the beginning, Mr. Bundy was planning what for his school?
3.   What did the students promise in order to get the ball out of the water?
4.   Who is the main character in this story?
5.   Mr. Bundy called a magician. What is the magician's first name?
6.   Mr. Bundy was changed into a _____.
7.   How did Mr. Bundy get back to being himself?
8.   Who was Ms. Moore?
9.   What did Nancy have in the shoebox?
10.   What did Mr. Bundy rescue from the pond?
11.   What did the magician leave at home?
12.   What is the title of this book?

Comprehension

1. Do you think Mr. Bundy was a good principal? Explain.
2. Summarize the problem.
3. Summarize the solution.

Application

1. What would you do if your principal turned into a frog?
2. Explain how you feel about a broken promise.
3. What was your favorite part of this story?
4. Calculate how many days Mr. Bundy was a frog.

Synthesis

1. What would have happened if the magician had not left his instruction book at home?
2. How would the story change if Mr. Bundy wasn't hit on the head with the ball?

Teacher's Notes:

The Frog Principal
by Stephanie Calmenson
Pattern

Cut out 12 ties for the comprehension questions.
Print a different question on each tie.

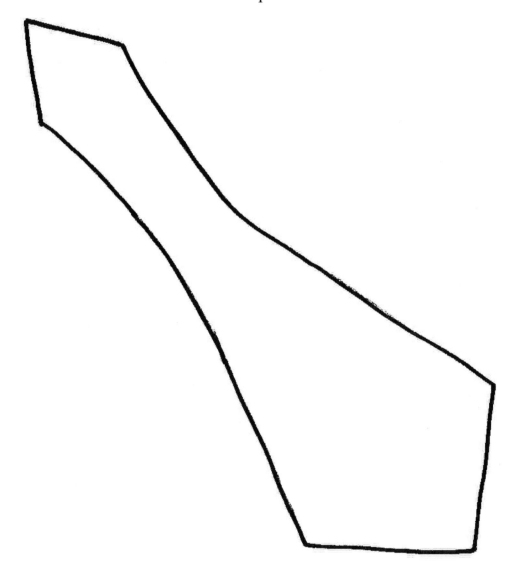

The Frog Principal
by Stephanie Calmenson
Worksheet

Write a letter to your principal telling what a wonderful job he or she is doing. Use the tie pattern below as the paper.

12
Maxwell's Magic Mix-Up

By Linda Ashman

From Linda Ashman. *Maxwell's Magic Mix-Up*. New York: Simon & Schuster Books for Young Readers, 2001.

Language Arts National Standards

NL-ENG.K-12.3 Evaluation Strategies

Students apply a wide range of strategies to comprehend, interpret, evaluate, and appreciate texts. They draw on their prior experience, their interactions with other readers and writers, their knowledge of word meaning and of other texts, their word identification strategies, and their understanding of textual features (e.g., sound-letter correspondence, sentence structure, context, graphics).

NL-ENG.K-12.11 Participating in Society

Students participate as knowledgeable, reflective, creative, and critical members of a variety of literacy communities.

Skills   Reading comprehension

Objective

Students will be able to play the "Who Am I" game by drawing on their recall of the story to decide which character fits the question. They also will be able to complete the worksheet about the key points in the story.

Grade Level   Second grade

Costume
Top hat
Black suit jacket
Magic wand

Props
Six party gift bags
Rock
Small broom
Small stuffed pig, cat, bird, clown

Materials   Name cards: Dad, Katie, Peter, Clown, Joey, and Louise

Instructions

Decorate the name cards to make them look like party place cards, only larger.

Use stickers or pictures of birthday balloons to make the cards kid-friendly.

Lesson

Step 1: Arrange the party packages ahead of time with the rock, pig, cat, broom, bird, and clown each in a different bag. Have name cards ready to spread out when playing the game at the end of the story. Introduce the story by waving the magic wand and state that all of the students are now at a big birthday party. Point out that this is the theme of this book.

Step 2: Read the story aloud.

Step 3: Lay out the name cards and explain the "Who Am I" game.

- Read a clue.
- Students will come up and peek inside the bags to find the correct character.
- Each student shows the class, and they accept or reject the answer.
- Another student will come up and match the character to the name on the card. Younger students may need help in remembering what the names are on the cards.

Step 4: Explain the following worksheet. Read the questions below and the words in the box on the worksheet for younger students.

- **"Who Am I" Clues**

1. I am seven years old. I'm sad and upset. Maxwell the Magician works his magic on me first.

Who am I?

2. I'm loud and clumsy. Swooping down, I hit a lamp. My claws end up in Katie's hair.

Who am I?

3. I think Joey looks good enough to eat. "Meeeoow" is my favorite word. Chasing birds is my specialty.

Who am I?

4. I am angry. These kids are making so much noise.

Who am I?

5. Sweeping the floor, I rush around the room.

Who am I?

6. I am big. Eating is my favorite pastime. In this story, I gobble up chips, cheese, and cookies.

Who am I?

7. I make kids laugh. In the end, this is whom they would rather have at the next party.

Who am I?

Teacher's Notes:

Maxwell's Magic Mix-Up
by Linda Ashman
Worksheet

Use the word box to answer the following questions.

1. The magician turns Louise into a _____.

2. Joey ends up a _____.

3. The magician's name is _____.

4. Who does the magician call to help him out of the mess?

_____.

5. The cat is _____.

6. How old is Louise? _____.

Word Box

• seven	• bird	• rock	• Maxwell	• nephew	• Kate

What happens at the end of this story?

_____

_____

_____

_____

Maxwell's Magic Mix-Up
by Linda Ashman
Pattern

Cut out five party hats from bright colored paper and
decorate them with stickers and magic markers. Adjust the
pattern as needed. Form the hats into cones and staple them.
Use hot glue to attach them to the rock, stuffed animals,
and broom.

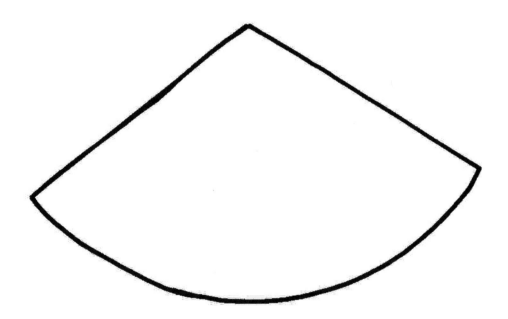

13
Franklin's Halloween

By Paulette Bourgeois

From Paulette Bourgeois. *Franklin's Halloween.* New York: Scholastic, 1996.

Language Arts National Standards

NL-ENG.K-12.3 Evaluation Strategies

Students apply a wide range of strategies to comprehend, interpret, evaluate, and appreciate texts. They draw on their prior experience, their interactions with other readers and writers, their knowledge of word meaning and of other texts, their word identification strategies, and their understanding of textual features (e.g., sound-letter correspondence, sentence structure, context, graphics).

NL-ENG.K-12.12 Applying Language Skills

Students use spoken, written, and visual language to accomplish their own purposes (e.g., for learning, enjoyment, persuasion, and the exchange of information.

Skills   Reading comprehension
Creative writing

Objective

Students will be able to answer the questions at the end of the story and then write a story about what they would have done if they had attended the party.

Grade Level   First and second grades

Props   White construction paper
One trick-or-treat plastic bag (to hold the questions)

Instructions

Cut out a ghost for each of the questions, using the pattern on the worksheet.

Lesson

Step 1: Read the story aloud and share the pictures.

Step 2: Students may come up one at a time to draw the questions from the trick-or-treat bag. Discuss the story as the questions are answered. Students can name a friend to help with the answer if they get stuck.

Step 3: Brainstorm ideas for student stories. Make a list on the board.

Step 4: Writing time (see worksheet).

Step 5: Form a circle and share the stories that have been written.

Questions Labeled with Bloom's Levels of Thinking Taxonomy

Knowledge

1. What did Franklin pick to be on Halloween?
2. Who was sick and didn't get to go to the party?
3. Where were Franklin and his friends afraid to visit?
4. Who was in charge of the haunted house?
5. Who is the main character in the story?

Comprehension

1. Explain why the ghost costume was a good choice for Mr. Owl.
2. Summarize the activities that took place at the party.
3. Explain to the class at what time of the year this story takes place and how the reader knows that.
4. Predict what will happen the day after Halloween when Franklin and his friends return to school.

Application

1. How did Franklin solve the mystery of the ghost?
2. Did the characters in the story show they were creative in the costumes that they chose to wear?
3. Have you ever been afraid on Halloween when you have gone out for trick or treat?

Teacher's Notes:

Franklin's Halloween
by Paulette Bourgeois and Brenda Clark
Worksheet

Write on the ghost what you would wear to Franklin's party.

14
Cobweb Christmas

By Shirley Climo

From Shirley Climo. *Cobweb Christmas*. [New York]: HarperCollins, 2001.

Language Arts National Standards

NL-ENG.K-12.3 Evaluation Strategies

Students apply a wide range of strategies to comprehend, interpret, evaluate, and appreciate texts. They draw on their prior experience, their interactions with other readers and writers, their knowledge of word meaning and of other texts, their word identification strategies, and their understanding of textual features (e.g., sound-letter correspondence, sentence structure, context, graphics).

NL-ENG.K-12.11 Participating in Society

Students participate as knowledgeable, reflective, creative, and critical members of a variety of literacy communities.

NL-ENG.K-12.1 Reading for Perspective

Students read a wide range of print and nonprint texts to build an understanding of texts, of themselves, and of the cultures of the United States and the world; to acquire new information; to respond to the needs and demands of society and the workplace; and for personal fulfillment. Among these texts are fiction and nonfiction, classic and contemporary works.

Skills	Reading comprehension

Objective

The students will be able to answer the questions at the end of the story.

Grade Level	First and second grades
Costume	Old looking shawl or a piece of wool. Apron Broom
Props	Small Christmas tree Sprig of greens for the catnip Plastic spiders and something to look like the webs that they will spin at the end of the story. Flannel pieces (see patterns) Christmas ornament hooks

Instructions

Using the patterns, cut cookies, the apple, the bone, and oats out of the felt.

Lesson

Step 1: Read the story aloud, dressed up as the little old lady. Ask students to listen for things that are different from the way they celebrate Christmas.

Step 2: Spend some time with the students pointing out which features in what they heard were different about Christmas traditions. *Example:* Kris Kringle and the filling of the shoes instead of the stockings.

Step 3: Lay out the flannel ornaments.

Step 4: As you read the questions, let students come up and pick ornaments to put on the tree. Match items like the bag of oats for the donkey and goat question where they apply.

Step 5: Complete the decorating by appointing students to be spiders and have them act out the part of the story where the spiders come inside and spin their webs on the tree branches.

Closure

See the author's note at the close of the book and explain the tradition of tinsel.

Questions Labeled with Bloom's Levels of Thinking Taxonomy[*]

First Grade Questions

Knowledge

1. What is the title of this story?*
2. Who is the main character?*
3. What country did Tante live in?
4. Why did she have to stand on a stool to get into bed?
5. What does Tante mean in German?
6. What animals lived with the old woman?*
7. What animals lived in the barn?*
8. When did Tante really clean her tiny cottage?
9. What did Tante go to the woods to chop down?*
10. What did Tante bake to put on her tree?*
11. What did she rub until they gleamed like glass?
12. What did she put on the tree for the cat?*
13. Who was Kris Kringle?*
14. What did people put by their doors for Kris Kringle to tuck gifts into?
15. Who let the spiders inside to see the Christmas tree?*

Comprehension

1. Contrast the Christmas customs of Germany and America.
2. Estimate how many spiders came in to see Tante's tree.
3. Describe Tante. How did the author let the reader know what she looked like?
4. Summarize what Tante did to prepare for the Christmas season.
5. Explain what Tante wanted for Christmas. Was this an unusual wish?

Application

1. Does this story remind you of a special Christmas that you spent with your family?
2. Calculate how long it must have taken for Tante to get ready for Christmas. Make a list and include the time for each event.

* = Questions for younger children.

Cobweb Christmas
by Shirley Climo
Pattern

Cut several shapes out of the
lighter felt to resemble cookies.

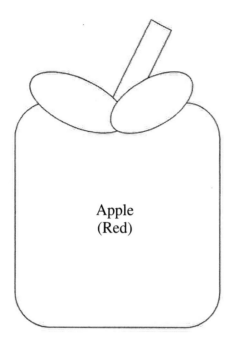

Apple
(Red)

Cut shapes from red, brown, and tan construction paper for students to use to create Tante's Christmas tree.

Basket of Oats
(Brown)

Oats

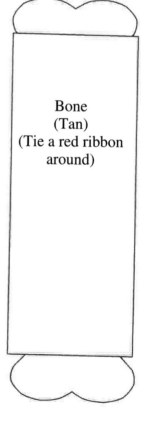

Bone
(Tan)
(Tie a red ribbon around)

15
Mrs. Piccolo's Easy Chair

By Jean Jackson

From Jean Jackson. *Mrs. Piccolo's Easy Chair.* New York: DK Publishing, 1999.

Language Arts National Standards

NL-ENG.K-12.3 Evaluation Strategies

Students apply a wide range of strategies to comprehend, interpret, evaluate, and appreciate texts. They draw on their prior experience, their interactions with other readers and writers, their knowledge of word meaning and of other texts, their word identification strategies, and their understanding of textual features (e.g., sound-letter correspondence, sentence structure, context, graphics).

NL-ENG.K-12.11 Participating in Society

Students participate as knowledgeable, reflective, creative, and critical members of a variety of literacy communities.

Skills	Reading comprehension

Objective

The students will be able to answer the questions at the end of the story.

Grade Level	Kindergarten through second grade
Costume	Straw hat with a bee glued on top Green scarf Pink sweater or jacket
Materials	Blanket or piece of material big enough to drape over a chair Empty cheese puff bag Full bag of cheese puffs to treat students (because the chair's favorite food was cheese puffs).

Lesson

Step 1: Put on the costume and greet children as they come in the door. Introduce yourself as the main character in the book that will be read today. Review what it means to be the main character in the story.

Step 2: Read the book aloud and let the kids be the sound effects for the noise that the chair makes when he swallows up the people. It will give the students something special to listen for.

Step 3: Make a large chair by draping the pink blanket or material over a regular chair.

Step 4: Have students come one at a time to sit in the large pink chair and answer the questions.

Closure

Worksheet: Students will write answers on the chair picture.

Questions Labeled with Bloom's Levels of Thinking Taxonomy

Knowledge

1. Mrs. Piccolo needed to go to the _____
2. Who owned the grocery store?
3. What was the name of the grocery store?
4. Who did the chair swallow first?
5. Who climbed into the chair and started to jump up and down?
6. What did Mrs. Piccolo serve when her guest returned home?
7. What happened at the end of the story?
8. What snack did the chair like best?
9. How many bags of cheese puffs could the chair buy?
10. How many people did the chair swallow all together?

Comprehension

1. Describe the chair's adventure to the grocery store.
2. Do you think Mrs. Piccolo knew where the chair had been? Explain.
3. Describe the chair.

Analysis

1. What was the funniest part?
2. What was your favorite part?

Synthesis

1. Do you think the chair will go to the grocery store again? Explain
2. Tell the story from the policeman's point of view.
3. Pretend you were a shopper in the grocery store and describe your reaction to the chair.

Teacher's Notes:

Mrs. Piccolo's Easy Chair
by Jean Jackson
Worksheet

What did the easy chair swallow?
List the answers on the chair.
Color the chair.

16
D.W. the Picky Eater

By Marc Brown

From Marc Brown. *D.W. the Picky Eater*. Boston: Little, Brown, 1995.

Language Arts National Standards

NL-ENG.K-12.3 Evaluation Strategies

Students apply a wide range of strategies to comprehend, interpret, evaluate, and appreciate texts. They draw on their prior experience, their interactions with other readers and writers, their knowledge of word meaning and of other texts, their word identification strategies, and their understanding of textual features (e.g., sound-letter correspondence, sentence structure, context, graphics).

NL-ENG.K-12.11 Participating in Society

Students participate as knowledgeable, reflective, creative, and critical members of a variety of literacy communities.

Skills	Reading comprehension

Objective

Students will be able to distinguish between healthy and junk food by the end of the story.

Grade Level	First grade

Costume	Glasses Yellow shirt and red bow tie Jeans Round felt brown ears (cut out and glued onto a headband)

Props	Bag of plastic toy food from a toy store (salad items, milk, etc.) Box of frozen spinach (remove the spinach, wash the inside of the box and reseal. Brown chart paper cut to look like giant grocery bags (one labeled "junk," the other "healthy"). Magazine pictures of healthy and junk foods Small backpack Children's menu (see Instructions) Glue sticks and scissors

Instructions

Display the paper bags on a table so students can draw or glue pictures on them (see step 3 of the lesson). Make a children's menu from a folded piece of construction paper with pictures and words printed out for D. W. to look at. Be sure to include Little Bo Peep Pot Pie.

Lesson

Step 1: Dress up as Arthur and tell the story from the point of view of the big brother. The plastic food and menu should be inside the backpack; pull them out at the appropriate time in the story.

Step 2: Lead the students in a discussion of what D. W. liked and didn't like. Ask the students why D.W. was willing to try the "Little Bo Beep Pot Pie."

Step 3: Explain the bag activity. Each student will need to find a picture or draw one that would fit on each bag. (One healthy and one junk food item.) The students will create two giant bags with collage pictures. The students will glue one picture on the junk bag and one picture on the healthy bag.

Step 4: Worksheet: Circle all of the healthy foods so D.W. knows what she needs to eat.

Teacher's Notes:

Circle the things that are healthy so that D.W. knows what is good for her to eat.

Spinach	Potato chips
Cake	Candy
Salad	Spaghetti
Carrot Sticks	Milk

Little Bo Beep Pot Pie

List three healthy foods that you like to eat:

_____

_____

_____

17
The Bag I'm Taking to Grandma's

By Shirley Neitzel

From Shirley Neitzel. *The Bag I'm Taking to Grandma's*. New York: Scholastic, 1995.

Language Arts National Standards

NL-ENG.K-12.3 Evaluation Strategies

Students apply a wide range of strategies to comprehend, interpret, evaluate, and appreciate texts. They draw on their prior experience, their interactions with other readers and writers, their knowledge of word meaning and of other texts, their word identification strategies, and their understanding of textual features (e.g., sound-letter correspondence, sentence structure, context, graphics).

NL-ENG.K-12.11 Participating in Society

Students participate as knowledgeable, reflective, creative, and critical members of a variety of literacy communities.

Skills   Reading comprehension

Objective

Students will be able to complete the questions on the worksheet at the end of the story.

Grade Level   Second grade

Props   Two brown paper shopping bags with handles
                  Slippers and some boys' clothes (items that one would take when spending the night at Grandma's)
                  Matchbox cars, a mitt, a space rocket, toy animals "two by two," a bunny, a pillow, a book, and a flashlight (small enough so that all will fit inside the second shopping bag)

Instructions

Print the words "that I'll pack in the bag I'm taking to Grandma's" on the outside of both bags so that kids will be able to read the words as the story is read. Stuff the first bag with newspaper so that it will stand up on a table. The second bag is needed for all of the things that are mentioned in the story.

63

Lesson

Step 1: Tell the story and explain that the kids will help out by reading the words, "that I'll pack in the bag I'm taking to Grandma's." Have the shopping bag with words displayed so that the students can easily read them. Use the props to aid in the telling. Pull them out one at a time as needed.

Step 2: After the story, let students place the items in two piles:

- Mother wants him to put away
- Mother thinks he can take

Closure

Give out the comprehension worksheet. Go over the questions and word box as needed for the class.

Teacher's Notes:

The Bag I'm Taking to Grandma's
By Shirley Neitzel

Word Box

• flashlight • car • books • slippers • mitt • bunny • pillow

1. What is needed to play ball? _____

2. What does the little boy sleep with at night? _____

3. What is fluffy and light? _____

4. Grandma has plenty of what to read? _____

5. He can only take one _____.

6. Mother picks out _____ and other clothes for the trip.

7. What is needed to shine on the book? _____

Make a list of things you take when you visit your Grandma:

_____

_____

_____

_____

_____

_____

18
Strega Nona Takes a Vacation

By Tomie dePaola

From Tomie dePaola. *Strega Nona Takes a Vacation*. New York: Putnam, 2000.

Language Arts National Standards

NL-ENG.K-12.3 Evaluation Strategies

Students apply a wide range of strategies to comprehend, interpret, evaluate, and appreciate texts. They draw on their prior experience, their interactions with other readers and writes, their knowledge of word meaning and of other texts, their word identification strategies, and their understanding of textual features (e.g., sound-letter correspondence, sentence structure, context, graphics).

NL-ENG.K-12.11 Participating in Society

Students participate as knowledgeable, reflective, creative, and critical members of a variety of literacy communities.

Skills	Reading comprehension

Objective

Students will be able to listen to the story and then answer the questions. They will be able to relate the story to going on vacation with their own families.

Grade Level	Kindergarten through second grade
Costume	White apron White scarf for head
Props	Small suitcase or large handbag made from tapestry-type fabric
Materials	Wallpaper book with flowery samples Construction paper for backing the suitcase cutouts Postcards or pictures from the beach

Instructions

Cut out one of the small suitcases for each question (see the pattern).

Lesson

Step 1: Greet students in costume. Ask who likes to go on vacation. Allow time to share. Students will enjoy telling where they have been. Share pictures about the beach and introduce the book. Explain that the main character is going on a vacation.

Step 2: Read the story aloud.

Step 3: Select students one at a time to read the questions from the small suitcase or large handbag

Closure

Students will draw pictures of their favorite vacations. Have students draw on one side of the paper and label the place they visited on the other side. Collect pictures and combine into a class book using the title "Guess Where I Have Been."

Questions Labeled with Bloom's Levels of Thinking Taxonomy

Knowledge

1. Who is the main character in this book?
2. What chores could Big Anthony do for Strega Nona while she was on vacation?
3. What could Bambolona do to help while Strega Nona was on vacation?
4. What did Strega Nona send Big Anthony?
5. What did Strega Nona send Bambolona?
6. Who took the message to Strega Nona about the problems at home?

Comprehension

1. Summarize the trouble over the presents that Strega Nona sent.
2. Predict where Strega Nona will go next on her vacation.
3. Explain why the villagers felt Strega Nona should go on a vacation.
4. Describe what Strega Nona did on her vacation.

Application

1. Does this story remind you of a trip that you went on with your family? Describe it for the class.
2. Did Strega Nona solve the problem over her next vacation? How do you feel about Big Anthony staying out of trouble?

Teacher's Notes:

Strega Nona Takes a Vacation
by Tomie dePaola
Pattern

Cut out a handbag for each of the questions.
Use an old wallpaper book or flowery
wrapping paper that looks like Strega
Nona's bag. Laminate before using.

19
The Rainbow Fish

By Marcus Pfister

From Marcus Pfister. *The Rainbow Fish*. New York: North South Books, 1992.

Language Arts National Standards

NL-ENG.K12.3 Evaluation Strategies

Students apply a wide range of strategies to comprehend, interpret, evaluate, and appreciate texts. They draw on their prior experience, their interactions with other readers and writers, their knowledge of word meaning and of other texts, their word identification strategies, and their understanding of textual features (e.g., sound-letter correspondence, sentence structure, context, graphics).

NL-ENG.K-12.5 Communication Strategies

Students employ a wide range of strategies as they write and use different writing process elements appropriately to communicate with different audiences for a variety of purposes.

NL-ENG.K-12.12 Applying Language Skills

Students use spoken, written, and visual language to accomplish their own purposes (e.g., for learning, enjoyment, persuasion, and the exchange of information).

Skills   Comprehension

Objective

Students will be able to answer questions related to the story.

Grade Level   Second grade

Props   A stick with string and magnet attached (for a fishing pole)
Blue piece of material or child's wading pool for water
Paper clips for fishhooks

Materials   A copy of a fish picture for each student
Scrap paper and pencils
Crayons
Silver wrapping paper
Goldfish crackers

Lesson 1

Step 1: Read the story and discuss characters, setting, problem, and solution. Write a good comprehension question model for the students. *Example:* Explain how you had to share something like Rainbow Fish.

Step 2: Allow time for students to write one or two questions.

Lesson 2

Step 1: Students will color their fish and leave one scale blank. Have them cut out a piece of silver paper to fit the blank scale and glue it in place.

Step 2: Students will write questions on the back of the fish, or they can type their questions on the computer, print them out, and trim them to fit the back of the fish, then glue them on. Have them place a paper clip near the mouth of the fish.

Lesson 3

Step 1: Play a fishing game. Students take turns fishing and answering questions.

Step 2: Treat students to Goldfish crackers.

Modifications for kindergarten and first grade: Prepares the questions and place them on the backs of the fish. Play the game and give out fish crackers.

Questions Labeled with Bloom's Levels of Thinking Taxonomy

Knowledge

1. Who is the main character in the story?
2. How did Rainbow Fish feel in the beginning of the story?
3. What did Rainbow Fish look like in the beginning of the story?
4. What was wrong with Rainbow Fish in the beginning of the story?
5. Who were the other characters in the story?
6. What was the setting for the story?
7. Whom did Rainbow Fish visit?
8. What did the octopus say to Rainbow Fish?
9. What did Rainbow Fish do at the end of the story?
10. How did Rainbow Fish feel at the end of the story?

Comprehension

1. Describe Rainbow Fish at the beginning of the story.
2. Describe Rainbow Fish in the middle of the story.
3. Describe Rainbow Fish at the end of the story.
4. Summarize the problem in the story.
5. Summarize the solution in the story.

Application

1. How do you feel about how the other fish treated Rainbow Fish?
2. Explain how you have had to share something like Rainbow Fish did.

Analysis

1. Why was the octopus wise?

Synthesis

1. What would have happened if Rainbow Fish had not shared his scales?

Evaluation

1. What was your favorite part of the story?

Teacher's Notes:

20
Timothy Goes to School

By Rosemary Wells

From Rosemary Wells. *Timothy Goes to School.* New York: Penguin Group, 2000.

Language Arts National Standards

NL-ENG.K12.3 Evaluation Strategies

Students apply a wide range of strategies to comprehend, interpret, evaluate, and appreciate texts. They draw on their prior experience, their interactions with other readers and writers, their knowledge of word meaning and of other texts, their word identification strategies, and their understanding of textual features (e.g., sound-letter correspondence, sentence structure, context, graphics).

NL-ENG.K-12.5 Communication Strategies

Students employ a wide range of strategies as they write and use different writing process elements appropriately to communicate with different audiences for a variety of purposes.

NL-ENG.K-12.12 Applying Language Skills

Students use spoken, written, and visual language to accomplish their own purposes (e.g., for learning, enjoyment, persuasion, and the exchange of information).

Skills	Comprehension
	Identification of color words

Objective

Students will be able to answer the comprehension questions at the end of the story. Students will also be able to identify color words as an additional activity.

Grade Level	Kindergarten
Props	Pencil box to hold questions
Materials	Construction paper (red, green, blue, orange, purple, and yellow)

Instructions

Cut several of the crayon shapes out of the construction paper and write questions on them.

Lesson

Step 1: Introduce the story, author, and illustrator.

Step 2: Read the story and draw attention to the colors in the story.

73

Step 3: Students will draw questions out of the box, answer them, and identify the colors of the crayons.

Step 4: **Worksheet:** Students will find color words in the word search and color crayon.

Crayon Pattern

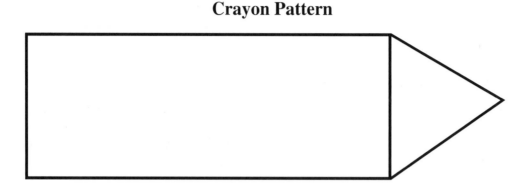

Questions Labeled with Bloom's Levels of Thinking Taxonomy

Knowledge

1. Where did Timothy go?
2. What did Timothy take to school?
3. Who was Timothy's new classmate?
4. What color was Timothy's new jacket?
5. Who made Timothy's clothes?
6. What kind of animal was Timothy?
7. Who became Timothy's friend at the end of the story?
8. What color is like Violet's name?

Comprehension

1. Why did Timothy and Violet become friends?
2. Why did the teacher say Timothy and Claude would be the best of friends?
3. How did Timothy feel at the beginning of the story?
4. How did Timothy feel at the middle of the story?
5. How did Timothy feel at the end of the story?
6. What grade was Timothy in? Explain

Application

1. Are you like Timothy or Claude? Explain

Analysis

1. What was your favorite part of the story?

Timothy Goes to School
by Rosemary Wells
Worksheet

RED

BLUE

YELLOW

GREEN

PURPLE

ORANGE

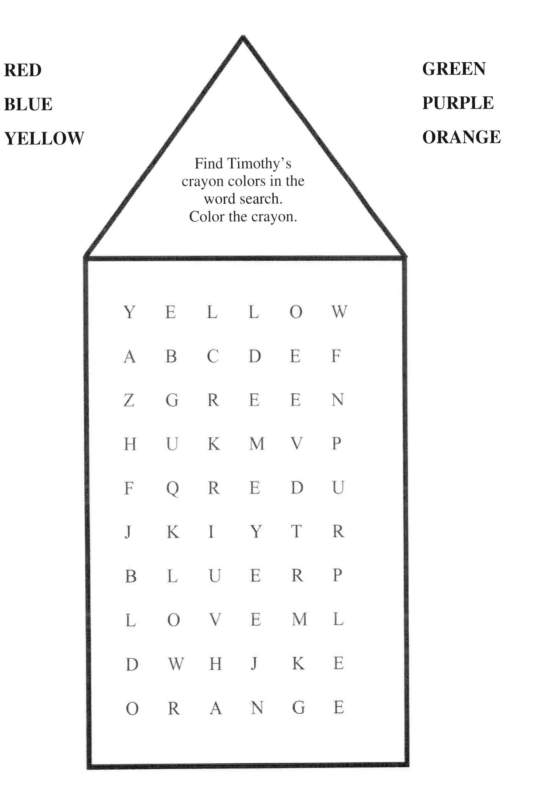

Find Timothy's
crayon colors in the
word search.
Color the crayon.

Y	E	L	L	O	W
A	B	C	D	E	F
Z	G	R	E	E	N
H	U	K	M	V	P
F	Q	R	E	D	U
J	K	I	Y	T	R
B	L	U	E	R	P
L	O	V	E	M	L
D	W	H	J	K	E
O	R	A	N	G	E

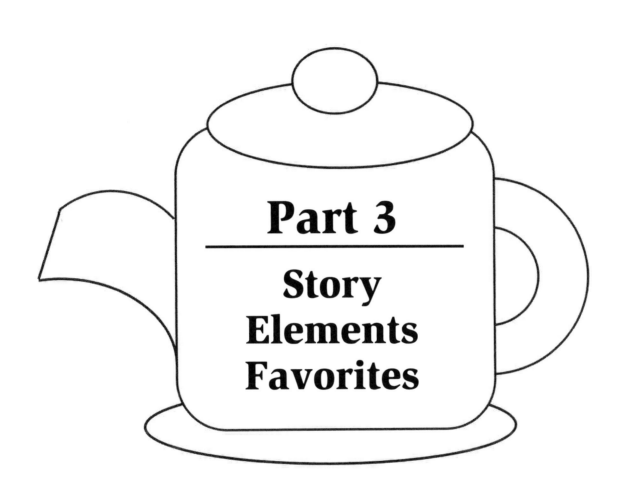

Part 3
_____

**Story
Elements
Favorites**

21
Bark, George

By Jules Feiffer

From Jules Feiffer. *Bark, George*. New York: HarperCollins, 1999.

Language Arts National Standards

NL-ENG.K-12.1 Reading for Perspective

Students read a wide range of print and nonprint texts to build understanding of texts, of themselves, and of the cultures of the United States and the world; to acquire new information; to respond to the needs and demands of society and the workplace; and the personal fulfillment. Among these texts are fiction and nonfiction, classic and contemporary works.

NL-ENG.K-12.3 Evaluation Strategies

Students apply a wide range of strategies to comprehend, interpret, evaluate, and appreciate texts. They draw on their prior experience, their interactions with other readers and writers, their knowledge of word meaning and of other texts, their word identification strategies, and their understanding of textual features (e.g., sound-letter correspondence, sentence structure, context, graphics).

Skills	Elements of the story Main and supporting characters

Objective

Students will be able to identify the main and supporting characters in the story and be able to pick out the different animal characters and the words they speak.

Grade Level	First grade
Costume	Doctor's coat with pockets Name tag
Props	Dog puppet dressed in a child or infant size T-shirt Small stuffed cat, duck, pig, and cow (should be small so as to appear to be inside the dog as you pull them out of the shirt) Bigger stuffed dog for the mother, or a second puppet White surgical gloves
Materials	Word cards for main and supporting characters Word cards for the words that George said in the story (*meow, quack-quack, oink, moo,* and *hello*)

Lesson

Step 1: Dress as the doctor and tell the story from his viewpoint. Pretend to pull out the animals from the dog's mouth as the story unfolds. The pockets in the coat can be used to hide the props if your puppet isn't big enough to hold all of the stuffed animals.

Step 2: Introduce the words *main* and *supporting characters*. Use the word cards to help students become familiar with the words. Spend time defining the words and how they are used in the story format. As a group, have students recall the main and supporting characters from the story.

Step 3: Let students group, the props into main and supporting categories.

Closure

1. Post the words that George says and review which character in the story matches them.
2. Read the book and let the students be the voice of George. Follow up with the worksheet.
3. Leave the words posted so students can use them.

Teacher's Notes:

Bark, George
by Jules Feiffer
Worksheet

The main character in this story was _____.

Draw the animals that support the main character. Can you remember what sounds each animal makes? Write those under each drawing.

1.

2.

3.

4.

Word Box

| • Moo | • Oink | • Quack-quack | • Meow | • George |

22
Big Al

By Andrew Clements

From Andrew Clements. *Big Al.* New York: Simon & Schuster Books for Young Readers, 1988.

Language Arts National Standards

NL -ENG.K12.3 Evaluation Strategies

Students apply a wide range of strategies to comprehend, interpret, evaluate, and appreciate texts. They draw on their prior experience, their interactions with other readers and writers, their knowledge of word meaning and of other texts, their word identification strategies, and their understanding of textual features (e.g., sound-letter correspondence, sentence structure, context, graphics).

NL -ENG.K-12.11 Participating in Society

Students participate as knowledgeable, reflective, creative, and critical members of a variety of literacy communities.

Skills   Story elements (characters, setting, problem, and solution)

Objective

Students will be able to identify the characters, setting, problem, and solution in the story. Second grade students will also be able to write a story summary with minimum help from the teacher.

Grade Level   First and second grades

Materials   Two-sided tape
Magazine pictures or die cut pictures of a large fish, a small fish, and a sea
Large paper for summary chart
Copy of worksheet for each second grade student.

Instructions

Glue the pictures on 5-by-7-inch paper and laminate them. Write "Big Al" on the big fish, "little fish" on the picture of the little fish, and "sea" on the picture of the sea. (See example.)

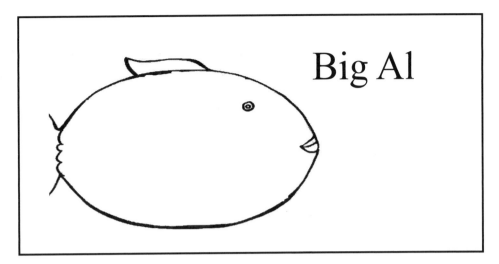

Example of Cards

Write the problem, the solution, and the author and title on the same size paper as the pictures and laminate that paper.

Enlarge the summary chart worksheet for the first grade activity and laminate it (see pattern).

First Grade Lesson

Step 1: Introduce the book.

Step 2: Display the summary chart and tell the students to listen for the characters, setting, problem, and solution in the story. Read the story aloud.

Step 3: **Group activity:** Pass out the papers with the pictures and words. Using the two-sided tape, students will place the pictures and words in the correct blocks on the summary chart.

Step 4: **Additional activity:** Students will enjoy racing to see who can place the items in the correct blocks the fastest.

Second Grade Lesson

Step 1: Introduce the story.

Step 2: Display the summary chart and tell the students to listen for characters, setting, problem, and solution in the story. Read the story aloud.

Step 3: After reading story, explain the worksheet and have students complete the summary.

Step 4: Have students share their summaries with the class.

Teacher's Notes:

Story Summary

Big Al
By Andrew Clements

The characters in the story are _____

_____

_____

_____.

The setting takes place in the _____

_____

_____

_____.

The problem in the story _____

_____

_____

_____.

The solution in the story _____

_____

_____

_____.

Big Al
by Andrew Clements
Summary Chart

Author
Title

Characters

Setting

Problem

Solution

23

Cindy Ellen: A Wild Western Cinderella

By Susan Lowell

From Susan Lowell. *Cindy Ellen: A Wild Western Cinderella*. [New York]: HarperCollins, 2000.

Language Arts National Standards

NL-ENG. K-12.1 Reading for Perspective

Students read a wide range of print and nonprint texts to build an understanding of texts, of themselves, and of the cultures of the United States and the world; to acquire new information; to respond to the needs and demands of society and the workplace; and for personal fulfillment. Among these texts are fiction and nonfiction, classic and contemporary works.

NL-ENG.K-12.2 Understanding the Human Experience

Students read a wide range of literature from many periods in many genres to build an understanding of many dimensions (e.g., philosophical, ethical, aesthetic) of human experience.

NL-ENG.K-12.12 Applying Language Skills

Students use spoken, written, and visual language to accomplish their own purposes (e.g., for learning, enjoyment, persuasion, and the exchange of information).

Skills   Elements of the story

Objective

Students will be able to point out the main character, setting, problem, and solution in this story. They will also be able to point out the things that are different about this version compared to the traditional Cinderella story.

Grade Level   Second grade

Costume   Western-type outfit

Materials   Dry eraser marker
Scrap paper, scissors, glue sticks, and worksheet vest for each student

Instructions

Enlarge the worksheet vest onto a poster size piece of paper. Clip it to the chalkboard in easy view of students' desks. Include the story element words that are on the worksheet. Decorate and laminate the large vest.

Lesson

Step 1: Ask students to listen for things that are different compared to the traditional Cinderella.

Step 2: Read the story aloud and share the pictures.

Step 3: Discuss the points that are different. Make a list on the black board.

Step 4: Using the vest worksheet, lead the discussion to cover all of the main elements in the story. Fill in the poster-size vest as students fill in their worksheets.

Closure

As time permits, allow students to cut out their vests and decorate them. Provide scrap paper for buttons and fringe.

Teacher's Notes:

Cindy Ellen: A Wild Western Cinderella
by Susan Lowell
Worksheet

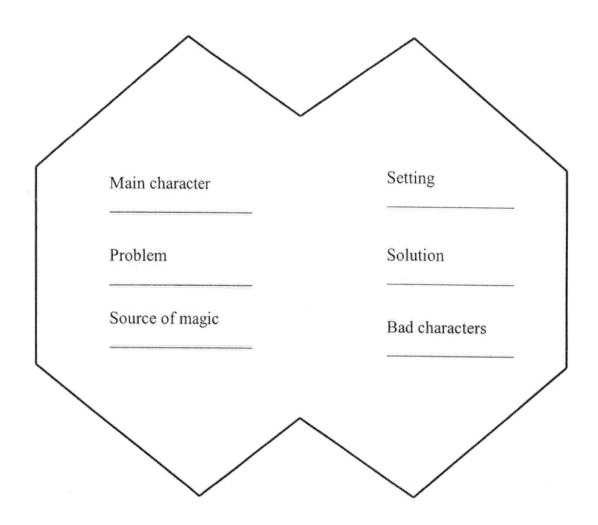

Main character
_____

Setting
_____

Problem
_____

Solution
_____

Source of magic
_____

Bad characters
_____

List the major story elements and decorate the vest.

24
The Lady with the Alligator Purse

By Nadine Bernard Westcott

From Nadine Bernard Westcott. *The Lady with the Alligator Purse.* Boston: Little, Brown, 1988.

Language Arts National Standards

NL-ENG.K12.3 Evaluation Strategies

Students apply a wide range of strategies to comprehend, interpret, evaluate, and appreciate texts. They draw on their prior experience, their interactions with other readers and writers, their knowledge of word meaning and of other texts, their word identification strategies, and their understanding of textual features (e.g., sound-letter correspondence, sentence structure, context, graphics).

NL-ENG.K-12.11 Participating in Society

Students participate as knowledgeable, reflective, creative, and critical members of a variety of literacy communities.

Skills	Story elements (characters, setting, problem, and solution)
	Dictionary skills (second grade)
	Career awareness

Objective

Students will be able to identify the characters, setting, problem, and solution. Second grade students will be able to look up and write a definition for a word in the dictionary, as a group with the teacher or librarian leading the activity. Students will be introduced to several careers and the skills needed for those careers.

Grade Level	Kindergarten through second grade

Props	Large green purse
	Stethoscope
	Nurse's hat (see pattern)
	Small empty pizza box
	Telephone
	Apron
	Baby doll
	Toy bathtub
	Bar of soap
	Two medicine bottles (labeled "penicillin" and "castor oil")
	Large shopping bag to store props

Materials
Construction paper (red, brown, and white)
Black marker
Red and brown chart paper
Dictionaries
Two-sided tape

Instructions: Preparing Materials

Make the nurse's hat. Using a regular piece of white paper, cut on the dotted lines and fold the two end pieces under the middle section, then staple.

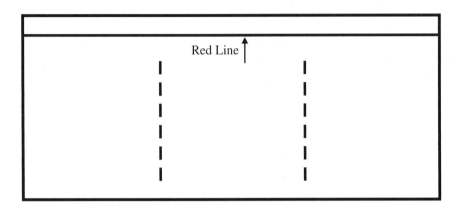

Cut circles from the red and brown paper for pepperoni and sausage. Cut rectangles from the white paper for the cheese. Write the characters, setting, problem, and solution on the pepperoni, sausage, and cheese. Enlarge the pizza pattern on red and brown chart paper. The brown paper is the outer circle, representing the crust, and the red paper is the inner circle, representing the pizza sauce. Write the words *characters, setting, problem,* and *solution* on parts of the pizza (see pattern).

Lesson

Step 1: Introduce the title, author, and book. Tell students they will need to find the characters, setting, problem, and solution.

Step 2: Tell the story using the props in the shopping bag. Pull items out of the bag as the story is told.

Step 3: Using two-sided tape, students will place the characters, setting, problem, and solution on the sections of the pizza. The characters and setting will be pepperoni and sausage and the problem and solution will be the cheese.

Step 4: Talk with the students about their favorite toppings for pizza. Kindergartners and first graders should complete worksheet K-1.

Step 5: Second graders will look up the words in the dictionary and write definitions on the lines (see Worksheet for Second Grade).

Step 6: **Additional lesson on careers:** Enlarge the career pattern onto chart paper or dry eraser board. Engage the students in a shared writing activity. Students will take turns writing the career skills on the paper or board. Begin by having the students identify the careers mentioned in the book. Ask questions such as: "What kind of education would one need for these jobs? What kind of skills do these careers need?" Students will take turns writing skills on the paper or board.

The Lady with the Alligator Purse
by Nadine Bernard Westcott
Worksheet for Second Grade

Dictionary Skills

Second Grade

1. Mumps _____

2. Measles _____

3. Penicillin _____

4. Castor Oil _____

5. Nonsense _____

The Lady with the Alligator Purse
by Nadine Bernard Westcott
Pattern

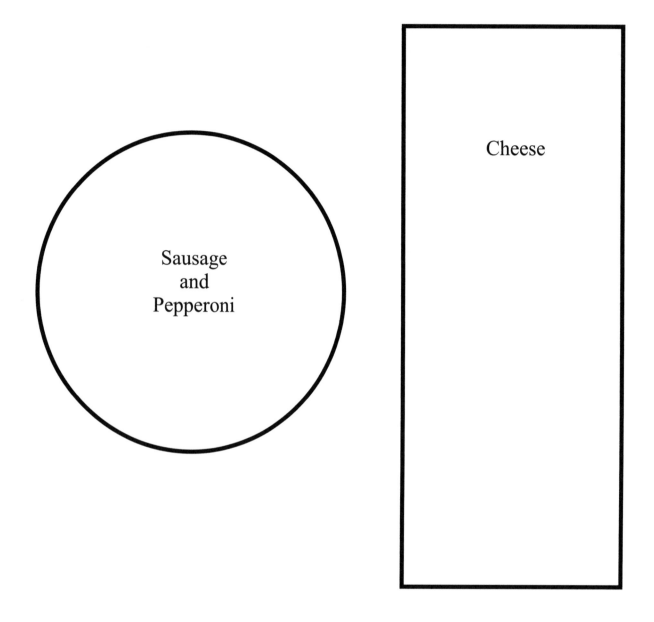

The Lady with the Alligator Purse
by Nadine Bernard Westcott
Pattern

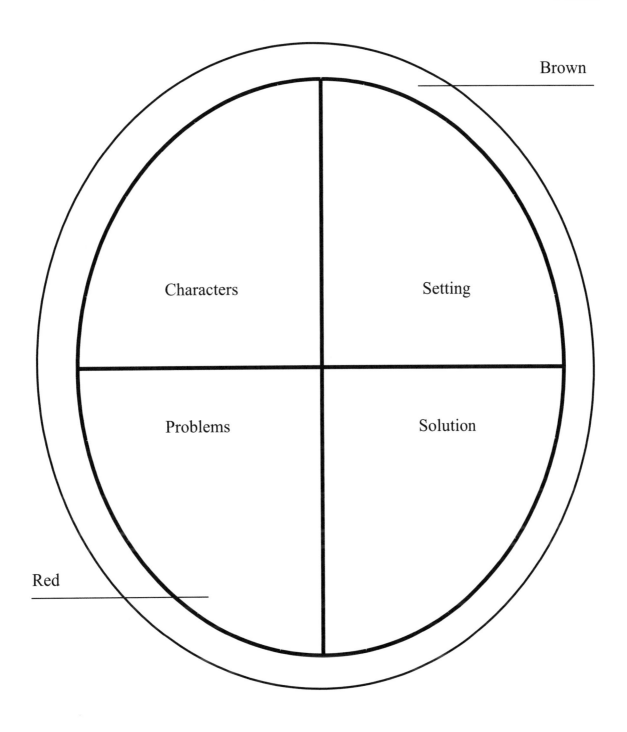

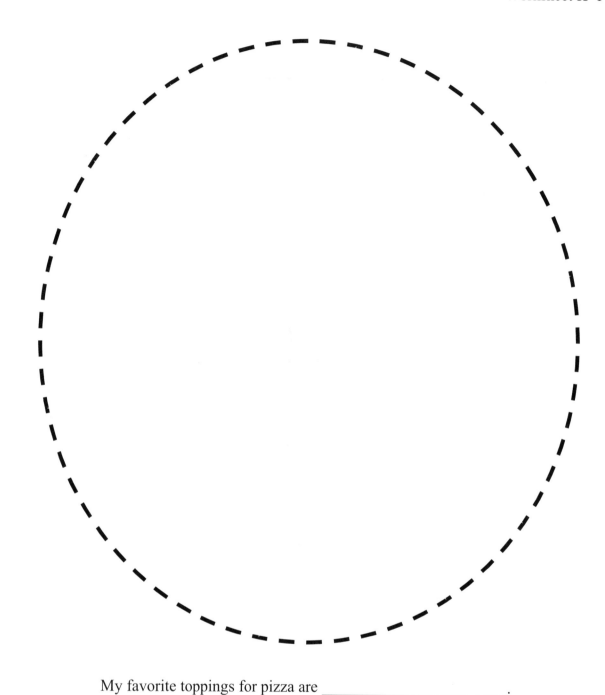

My favorite toppings for pizza are _____.

Pretend you are the lady with the alligator purse. Connect the dots and decorate the pizza.

The Lady with the Alligator Purse
by Nadine Bernard Westcott
Pattern: Career

Nurse | **Doctor**

Mother | **Pizza Delivery Person**

25
Grandpa's Teeth

By Rod Clement

From Rod Clement. *Grandpa's Teeth*. Sydney, Australia: HarperCollins, 1997.

Language Arts National Standards

NL-ENG.K12.3 Evaluation Strategies

Students apply a wide range of strategies to comprehend, interpret, evaluate, and appreciate texts. They draw on their prior experience, their interactions with other readers and writers, their knowledge of word meaning and of other texts, their word identification strategies, and their understanding of textual features (e.g., sound-letter correspondence, sentence structure, context, graphics).

NL-ENG.K-12.11 Participating in Society

Students participate as knowledgeable, reflective, creative, and critical members of a variety of literacy communities.

Skills	Story elements (characters, setting, problem, and solution) Parts of the library

Objective

Students will be able to identify the characters, setting, problem, and solution. Students will also be able to locate the parts of the library.

Grade Level	Kindergarten through second grade
Props	Denture cup
Materials	White construction paper Black marker

Instructions: Preparing Materials

Using the teeth patterns, make two different sizes of teeth. The small size is for the kindergarten questions and should fit in the denture cup. The larger size tooth is for the questions for the older students. Write questions on the teeth. The kindergarten teeth will have only one question on each. The teeth for the older students will have two questions. The first question will be about the story and the second will be a location in the library.

Lesson

Step 1: Introduce the title and author. Talk about the front cover of the book with the dentures. Discuss: "What are dentures?" Tell students to listen for the characters, setting, problem, and solution.

Step 2: Read the book aloud and talk about the story.

Step 3: Kindergarten students draw questions out of the denture cup and answer them.

Step 4: First and second grade students will go on a scavenger hunt. Hide the teeth in the library before class starts. Keep one tooth to start the game. A student will read the first question and answer. That student will pick another student to answer the second question. The answer to the second question leads the student to a location in the library where another tooth will be displayed. The teeth will be in plain sight, but students will have to answer the second question correctly to locate the next tooth. Continue answering questions and finding teeth until all teeth have been found.

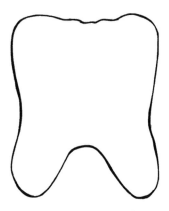

Small Tooth Pattern (Kindergarten)

Questions Labeled with Bloom's Levels of Thinking Taxonomy

Kindergarten

Knowledge
1. Who is the main character in the story?
2. Who are the other characters in the story?

Comprehension
1. Describe the setting for the story.
2. Summarize the problem in the story.
3. Summarize the solution in the story.

Application
1. What was your favorite part of the story?
2. How would you buy Grandpa's new teeth?

Analysis

1. How hard would it be to look in the dog's mouth?
2. What kind of food would you eat if you lost your teeth?
3. How old do you think Grandpa is? Why?

First and Second Grades

Knowledge

1. Who is the main character in the story?
2. In what part of the library would you find the book *Grandpa's Teeth?*
3. Who are the other characters in the story?
4. Where would you find a book about a dentist or police officer?

Comprehension

1. Describe the setting for the story.
2. Where would you find a book about how to be a dentist or police officer?
3. Summarize the problem in the story.
4. Where would you find a hard story book about teeth?
5. Summarize the solution in the story.
6. What do you use to help you find a book?

Application

1. What was your favorite part of the story?
2. What do we use to lookup information on the Internet?
3. How would you buy Grandpa's new teeth?
4. Who helps you in the library?

Analysis

1. How hard would it be to look in the dog's mouth?
2. Where would you find an up-to-date article about teeth and how to take care of teeth?
3. What kind of food would you eat if you lost your teeth?
4. Where would you take your books to check them out?
5. How old do you think Grandpa is? Why?
6. Where do we share a story as a class?

Teacher's Notes:

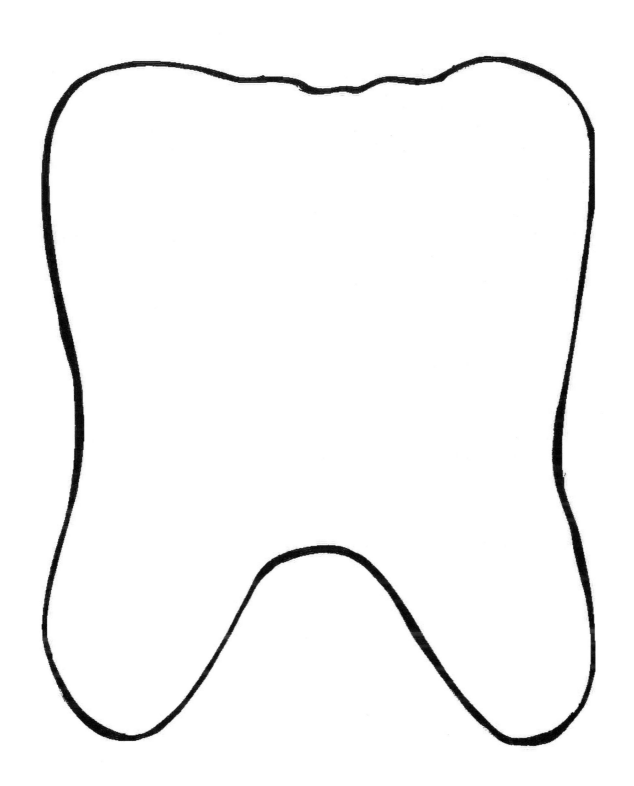

26
The Little Red Hen (Makes a Pizza)

By Philemon Sturges

From Philemon Sturges. *The Little Red Hen (Makes a Pizza).*
New York: Dutton Children's Books, 1999.

Language Arts National Standards

NL-ENG. K-12.1 Reading for Perspective

Students read a wide range of print and nonprint texts to build an understanding of texts, of themselves, and of the cultures of the United States and the world; to acquire new information; to respond to the needs and demands of society and the workplace; and for personal fulfillment. Among these texts are fiction and nonfiction, classic and contemporary works.

NL-ENG.K-12.2 Understanding the Human Experience

Students read a wide range of literature from many periods in many genres to build an understanding of many dimensions (e.g., philosophical, ethical, aesthetic) of human experience.

NL-ENG.K-12.12 Applying Language Skills

Students use spoken, written, and visual language to accomplish their own purposes (e.g., for learning, enjoyment, persuasion, and the exchange of information).

Skills	Elements of the story Compare and contrast

Objective

Students will be able to point out the main character, setting, problem and solution of this story. They will also be able to recall the traditional story of the little red hen and be able to compare and contrast the two stories.

Grade Level	First and second grades
Props	Traditional copy of the *Little Red Hen* Carry-out pizza box
Materials	Felt (tan), 14 inches square Red fabric paint for the tomato sauce Scrap felt (green, dark brown, yellow, and white for the topping of the pizza) Dictionaries for second grade

Instructions

Cut a large round circle from the felt square. Apply the red fabric paint with a small brush. Cut toppings from the scrap felt. Scatter and hot glue the toppings in place. Cut the finished pizza into five pieces. Prepare small signs that state *main character, setting, problem, solution*, and *ending*. Glue the signs onto the slices either on the front or the back.

Print and decorate word cards with pictures to use as a review at the end for the first grade class:

Word cards

Mozzarella cheese

Delicatessen

Supermarket

Hardware store

Anchovies

Lesson

Step 1: Start the lesson by showing the traditional version of the *Little Red Hen.* Let students retell the story as a way of getting them to focus on the main points of the story. Read the traditional version if the students are unfamiliar with the story.

Step 2: Show the new version and ask students to listen for things that are different.

Step 3: Read the story aloud.

Step 4: Share differences and similarities of these two stories. Students will see the easier ones but will need prompting regarding the others. Use the Little Red Hen Overhead for this part of the lesson. Use a dry eraser marker for easy clean up.

Closure

Build the pizza using the labeled pieces. This will be a good way to tie the lesson together. Point out how the author used the traditional story to create a more modern looking hen, and the setting is in a city rather than on a farm. The unexpected ending is another point to discuss. Students are surprised that the animals help do the dishes. Discuss why the other characters agree to help.

First Grade

Bring out the pizza box with word cards inside. Talk about the words in this story that might not be familiar to the students. Decorate the word cards with pictures to help in this process.

Second Grade

Divide the students into groups and give each group a word from the story that might not be familiar to them. Give them directions regarding looking up the words that you have selected.. Possible words: *delicatessen, supermarket, hardware, anchovies, mozzarella,* and *mushrooms.*

Directions

1. Look up the word in the dictionary.
2. Read and then write out the definition.
3. Use the word in a sentence.
4. Make a small illustration of the word.
5. Bring it to the circle and share your group's work. Practice reading the definition and the sentence if your group is finished early.

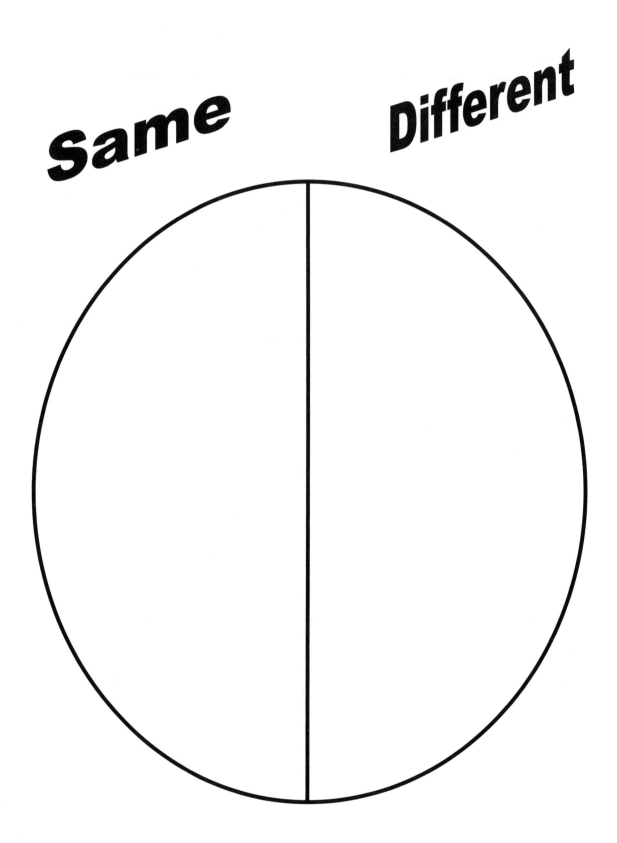

27
Miss Spider's Tea Party

By David Kirk

From David Kirk. *Miss Spider's Tea Party.* New York: Scholastic, 1994.

Language Arts National Standards

NL-ENG. K-12.1 Reading for Perspective

Students read a wide range of print and nonprint texts to build an understanding of texts, of themselves, and of the cultures of the United States and the world; to acquire new information; to respond to the needs and demands of society and the workplace; and for personal fulfillment. Among these texts are fiction and nonfiction, classic and contemporary works.

NL-ENG.K-12.12 Applying Language Skills

Students use spoken, written, and visual language to accomplish their own purposes (e.g., for learning, enjoyment, persuasion, and the exchange of information).

Skills   Elements of the story

Objective

Students will be able to point out the main character and setting of this story. They will also be able to act out the tea party and match up the characters with the numbers 1 through 12 as used in the text.

Grade Level   First and second grades

Costume   Black slacks
Long black knit top
Black panty hose (cut down so you have two long tubes that serve as the
     extra legs of a spider)

Props   Small plastic toy tea set
Table cloth
Plastic spiders and bugs

Materials   Six 8-by-10-inch placemats with words and pictures of moths, bumblebees,
     fireflies, beetles, violets, and ants on them (Stickers work well for this
     project.)
Five 8-by-10-inch size placemats with the numbers 1, 10, 8, 1, and 5 on them
Small cookie shapes for the numbers 2, 3, 4, 7, 6, 9, and 12
Small plate for the paper cookies

Instructions

Make the placemats and cookie shapes.

Stuff the panty hose with fiber fill or old panty hose cut up into small pieces. Pin the extra legs on to the black knit top. Use a large safety pin and pin them from underneath the shirt. In this manner you can add the legs without having to stitch them down.

Prepare room for the tea party. Spread the tablecloth out on the floor. Place the placemats around and set the tea set in the middle. Sprinkle the bugs and spiders around for effect.

Lesson

Step 1: Greet the students at the door dressed as a spider. Welcome them to the tea party and sit the guests around the tablecloth.

Step 2: Show the book and read it to the students. Ask students to listen for the way the author uses the numbers 1 through 12 in the story.

Step 3: Talk about the main character and the setting of this story. Students should be able to relate to these two elements because of the tea party and the way you are dressed. This can be a way of reinforcing these two elements.

Step 4: Pass the cookies out and ask the students to match them up with the placemats that have the insect pictures on them.

Step 5: Ask the students sitting near the numbered placemats to explain what the author used those numbers for.

Step 6: Optional: Have crackers or cookies to serve as a close out to story hour.

Leave the table items out and allow students to come and play tea party with the tea set and placemats.

Closure

First Grade

Design placemats for an imaginary tea party. Give each child a piece of construction paper the size of a regular placemat. Provide crayons and markers.

Second Grade

Use the worksheet to make up an invitation, stressing the following:

Who will be invited to your tea party?

What will you serve?

When will you have this party?

Where will the party take place?

Share placemats and invitations around the table setting.

Teacher's Notes:

Miss Spider's Tea Party
by David Kirk
Worksheet for Older Students

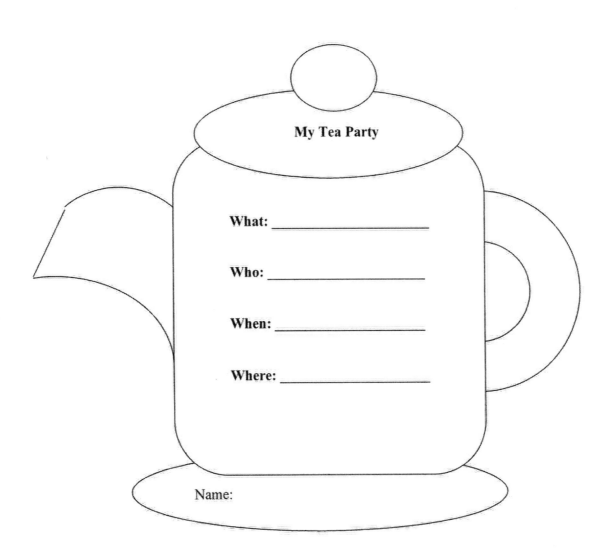

My Tea Party

What: _____

Who: _____

When: _____

Where: _____

Name:

Miss Spider's Tea Party
by David Kirk
Worksheet for Younger Students

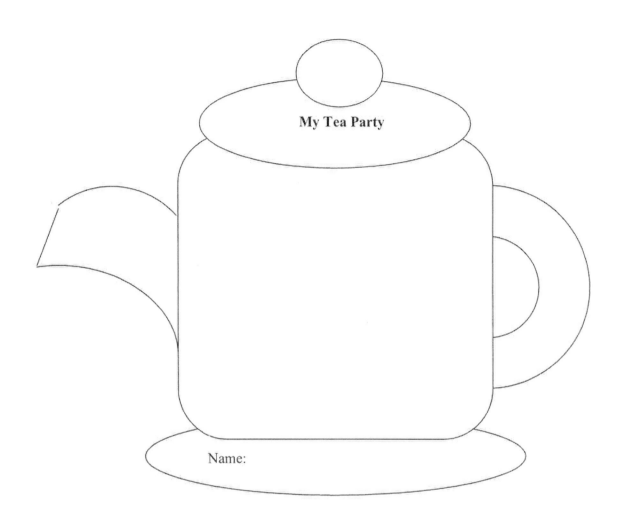

My Tea Party

Name:

Plan a tea party.
Draw the guest you will invite inside the teapot.

28
'Twas the Night Before Thanksgiving

By Dav Pilkey

From Dav Pilkey. *'Twas the Night Before Thanksgiving*. New York: Scholastic, 1990.

Language Arts National Standards

NL-ENG.K-12.11 Participating in Society

Students participate as knowledgeable, reflective, creative, and critical members of a variety of literacy communities.

NL-ENG.K-12.12 Applying Language Skills

Students use spoken, written, and visual language to accomplish their own purposes (e.g., for learning, enjoyment, persuasion, and the exchange of information).

Skills   Elements of the story
                  Compare and contrast

Objective

Students will be able to pick out the major elements of the story and compare and contrast this story to the Christmas version.

Grade Level   Second grade

Materials   Chart paper
                   'Twas the Night Before Christmas book
                   Felt in various colors (see patterns for colors)
                   Main character and *setting* word cards, printed out on paper backed with felt
                   Flannel board

Instructions

Using the patterns, cut out of the felt the items that students will use to create a big picture of the story.

Lesson

Step 1: Introduce the lesson by showing both books and talk about how the author used a traditional story, changed the main character and setting, and created a new story.

Step 2: Read the Thanksgiving story and share the pictures.

Step 3: Give each student a felt cutout that has been put together ahead of time. (See patterns for details.)

Step 4: Read the story a second time and explain that the students will create a big picture of this story. When the articles are mentioned the student with each piece should quietly come up and place it on the board (examples: house, turkey farm, Farmer Mac Nugget). Cut out extra leaves and food items so that each child will have a piece to place on the board. Stress that they need to be great listeners and also watch the illustrations for clues.

Closure

Setting and main character are the two story elements to stress in this story. Using the printed out word cards, place these on the picture with the item that denotes these elements: Main character: Farmer Mac Nugget; Setting: turkey farm.

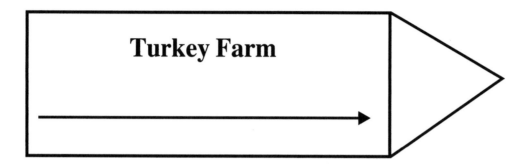

Lesson 2 Followup

Step 1: Review the Thanksgiving story and ask students to listen for the parts of *'Twas the Night Before Christmas* that are different.

Step 2: Make a chart of the things that are different in these two books. Using this time, compare and contrast the two stories, pointing out that the basic format is the same.

Step 3: Brainstorm ideas for another story. List possible ideas on the board and have students pick one for a class chart story. Prepare a chart beforehand with a few phrases that are the same in both stories, e.g., 'Twas the night before _____ and all through the _____." Write a class chart story and illustrate it.

Story possibilities:

- 'Twas the night before summer vacation.
- 'Twas the night before the big math test.
- 'Twas the night before Valentine's Day

Teacher's Notes:

'Twas the Night Before Thanksgiving
by Dav Pilkey
Pattern

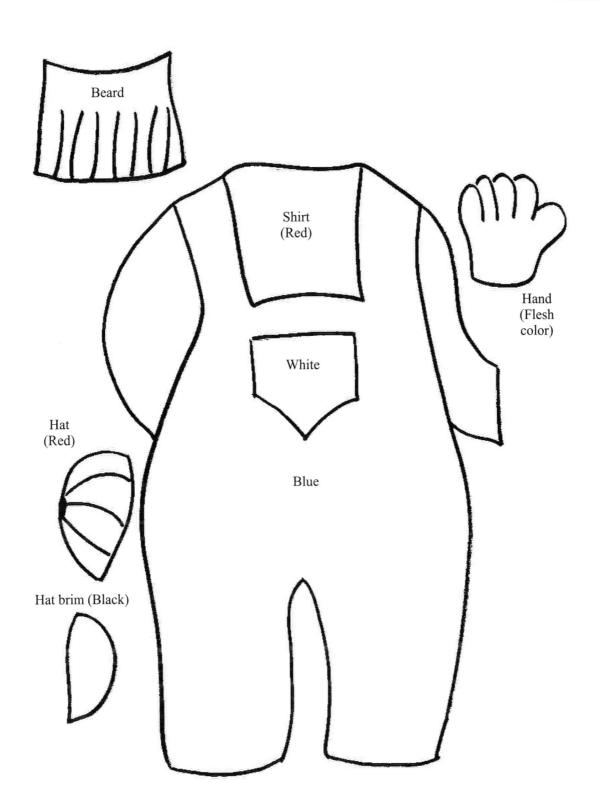

'Twas the Night Before Thanksgiving
by Dav Pilkey
Pattern

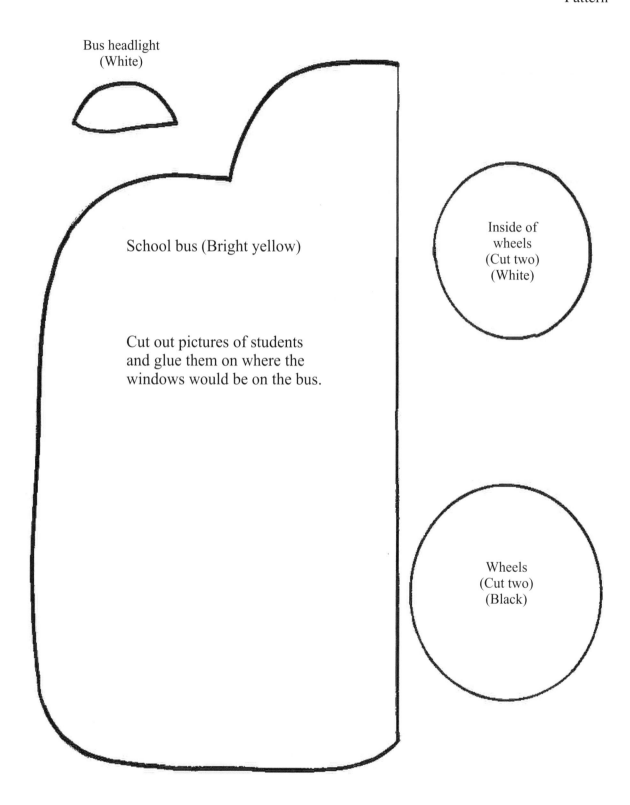

Bus headlight
(White)

School bus (Bright yellow)

Cut out pictures of students
and glue them on where the
windows would be on the bus.

Inside of
wheels
(Cut two)
(White)

Wheels
(Cut two)
(Black)

'Twas the Night Before Thanksgiving
by Dav Pilkey
Pattern

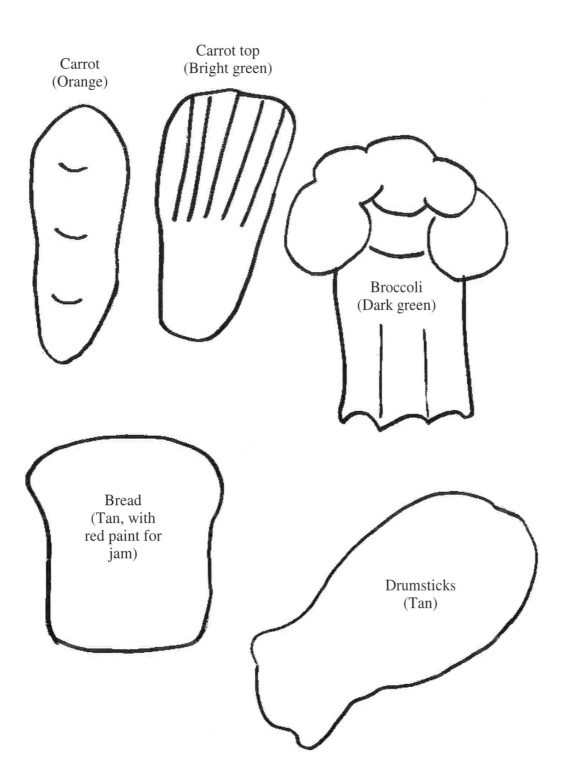

Carrot
(Orange)

Carrot top
(Bright green)

Broccoli
(Dark green)

Bread
(Tan, with
red paint for
jam)

Drumsticks
(Tan)

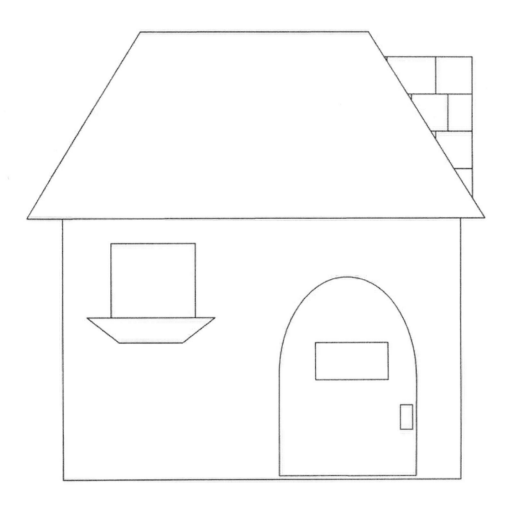

Farmer Mac Nuggett's house
Cut and glue together to make it as near to the story illustration as possible.

'Twas the Night Before Thanksgiving
by Dav Pilkey
Pattern

Turkey head
(Tan or Brown)

Boots
(Cut two)
(Black)

Body of turkey
(Brown)

Leaves
(Cut as many as
needed in fall
colors)

Glass of
water
(White)

Feet

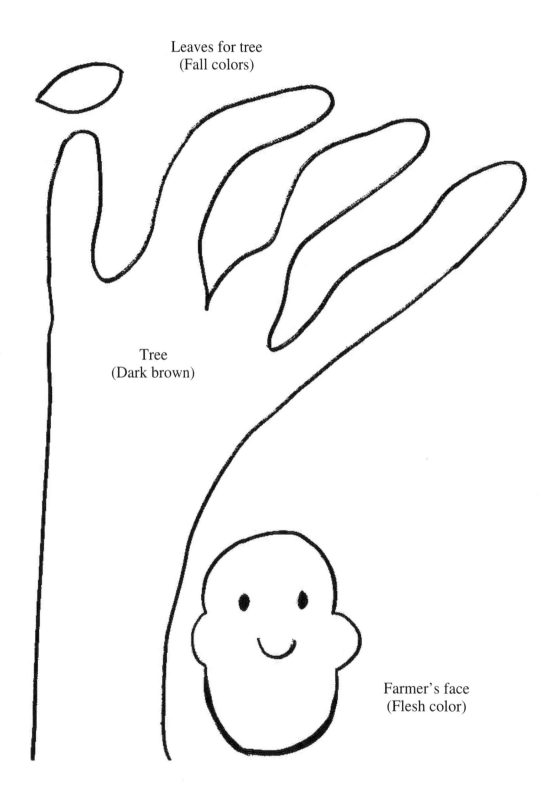

Leaves for tree
(Fall colors)

Tree
(Dark brown)

Farmer's face
(Flesh color)

29
When Winter Comes

By Nancy Van Laan

From Nancy Van Laan. *When Winter Comes.* New York: Atheneum Books for Young Readers, 2000.

Language Arts National Standards

NL-ENG. K-12.1 Reading for Perspective

Students read a wide range of print and nonprint texts to build an understanding of texts, of themselves, and of the cultures of the United States and the world; to acquire new information; to respond to the needs and demands of society and the workplace; and for personal fulfillment. Among these texts are fiction and nonfiction, classic and contemporary works.

NL-ENG.K-12.11 Participating in Society

Students participate as knowledgeable, reflective, creative, and critical members of a variety of literacy communities.

Skills   Elements of the story

Objective

Students will be able to point out the setting of this story and also illustrate the main sections to help create a wall mural

Grade Level   First grade

Materials   Long length of chart paper cut into eight equal pieces
Crayons

Instructions

Write on each piece of paper the seven questions that are asked in the story. The title and author should be written on the eighth piece. *Example:* "Where oh where do the leaves all go when winter comes and the cold wind blows?"

Lesson

Step 1: Ask the students to listen for things that explain the setting in this story. "How do you know that it is winter time and the story takes place outside?"

Step 2: Read the story and share the pictures with students.

Step 3: Go back to the introduction and discuss the questions that the students were asked at the beginning of the lesson. Students should mention (1) It is snowing on each page, (2) the people in the story are wearing coats, and (3) the title mentions the word "winter."

Closure

Divide the students into eight groups and give each a section of the mural. Explain that they are to illustrate the answers to the questions on their papers. Try to let the students do this from memory; don't let them go back to the book to see how the book illustrator completed each page. When the students are finished, collect the pieces and put them in order to form the story. Display them on a wall so that students can go back and read the whole story.

Teacher's Notes:

30
Show and Tell Bunnies

By Kathryn Lasky

From Kathryn Lasky. *Show and Tell Bunnies.* Cambridge, Mass.: Candlewick Press, 1998.

Language Arts National Standards

NL-ENG.K-12.3 Evaluation Strategies

Students apply a wide range of strategies to comprehend, interpret, evaluate, and appreciate texts. They draw on their prior experience, their interactions with other readers and writers, their knowledge of word meaning and of other texts, their word identification strategies, and their understanding of textual features (e.g., sound-letter correspondence, sentence structure, context, graphics).

NL-ENG.K12.12 Applying Language Skills

Students use spoken, written and visual language to accomplish their own purposes (e.g., for learning, enjoyment, persuasion and the exchange of information).

Skills	Character recognition
	Problem solving

Objective

Students will be able to identify the main character, the problem, the solution, and the setting of the story.

Grade Level	First and second grades

Costume	Pink sweatsuit
	Bunny ears
	White tail

Materials	Felt for bunny (see pattern)
	Buttons and trim for bunny shirt
	Paint for highlighting– (optional)
	Hot glue and glue gun
	Outdated wallpaper book from a local paint store
	Flannel board

Instructions

Cut felt bunny-shaped ears and attach them to a headband using hot glue or use a needle and heavy thread and a simple whip stitch. Using a five-inch circle cut out of cardboard, hot glue large cotton balls all over it to create a fluffy tail. Pin the tail onto your sweatpants. Paint whiskers on your face using a makeup pencil.

Lesson

Step 1: Read and share the book with students.

Step 2: Build a bunny on the flannel board while reviewing the story. Each piece can be a story element. Students will identify the elements and place them on the flannel board. A black marker will work on the felt.

Closure

Students can make bunnies from old wallpaper books or construction paper. Using the same patterns as for the felt bunnies, cut out some patterns from heavy paper for students to trace. This art project will require extra time, so carry it over to another library time or use as a center.

Teacher's Notes:

Show and Tell Bunnies
by Kathryn Lasky
Pattern

1.   Use the pattern pieces to cut bunny parts out of felt.

2.   Hot glue the hands and feet to the pants and shirt.

3.   Hot glue the eyes, nose, white face, and whiskers to the head of the bunny.

4.   Label the head, ears, shirt, and pants with the main points of the story.

Possible points: setting, call number, title, problem, and main character

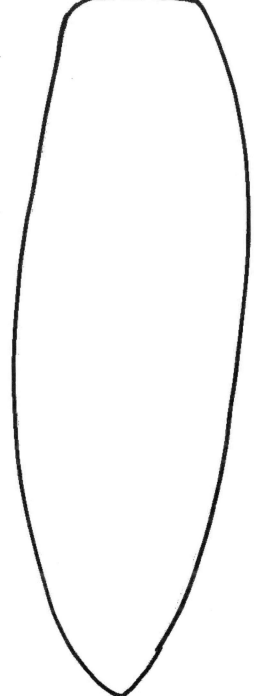

Show and Tell Bunnies
by Kathryn Lasky
Pattern

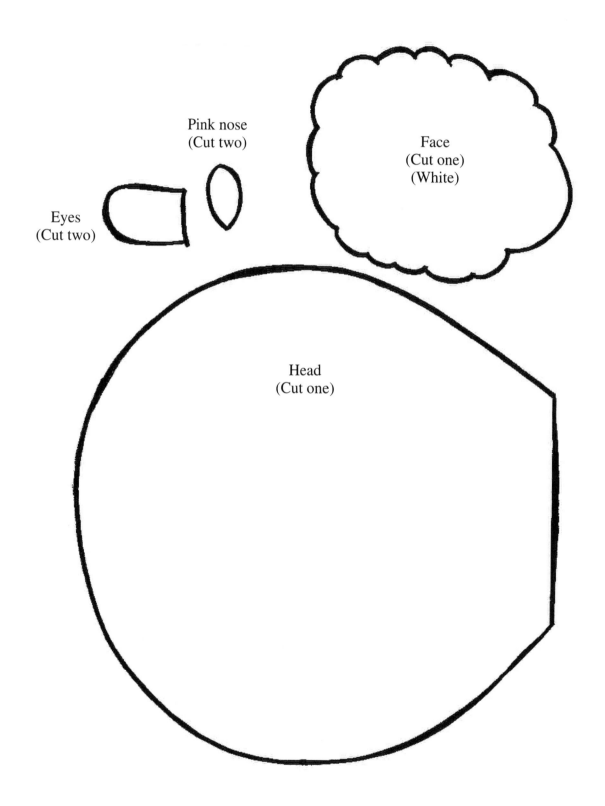

Eyes
(Cut two)

Pink nose
(Cut two)

Face
(Cut one)
(White)

Head
(Cut one)

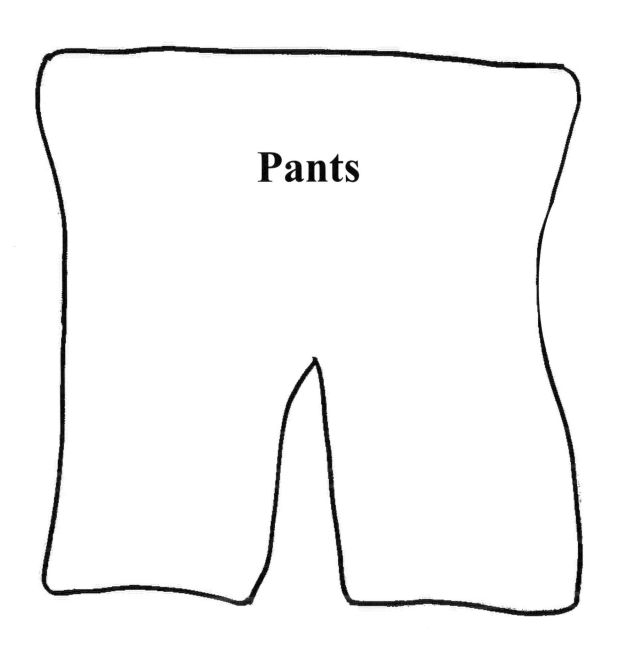

Pants

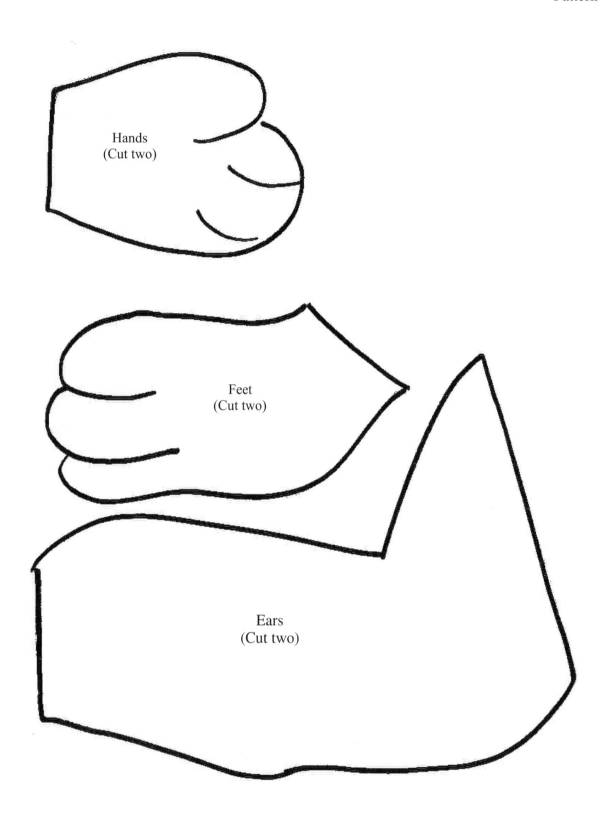

Hands
(Cut two)

Feet
(Cut two)

Ears
(Cut two)

Show and Tell Bunnies
by Kathryn Lasky
Pattern

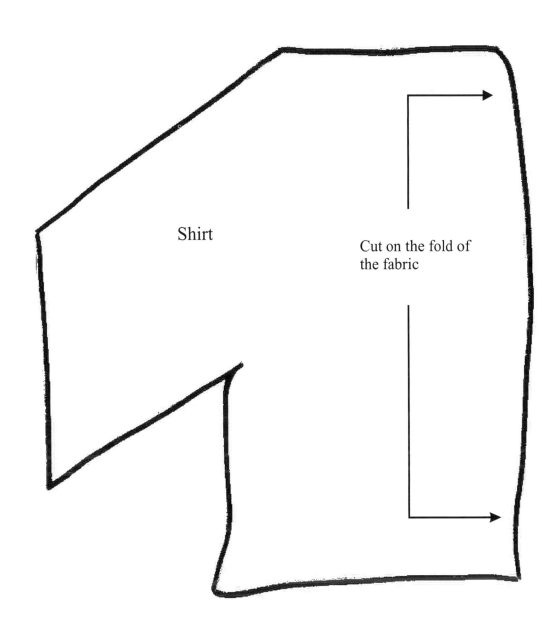

Shirt

Cut on the fold of
the fabric

Part 4

Author
Favorites

31

Eric Carle Study: *The Grouchy Ladybug* and *The Very Hungry Caterpillar*

By Eric Carle

From Eric Carle. *The Grouchy Ladybug.* New York: HarperCollins, 1977 (lessons 1 and 2);
The Very Hungry Caterpillar. New York: Philomel Books, 1987 (lesson 3).

LESSON 1

Language Arts National Standards

NL-ENG.K-12.1 Reading for Perspective

Students read a wide range of print and nonprint texts to build an understanding of texts, of themselves, and of the cultures of the United States and the world; to acquire new information; to respond to the needs and demands of society and the workplace; and for personal fulfillment. Among these texts are fiction and nonfiction, classic and contemporary works.

NL-ENG.K-12.3 Evaluation Strategies

Students apply a wide range of strategies to comprehend, interpret, evaluate, and appreciate texts. They draw on their prior experience, their interactions with other readers and writers, their knowledge of word meaning and of other texts, their word identification strategies, and their understanding of textual features (e.g., sound-letter correspondence, sentence structure, context, graphics).

Skills	Retelling
	Telling time

Objective

Students will be able to retell the story and also be able to understand the changing time of each event as it happens. Students will also observe the changes in size of the ladybug as compared to the other animals in the story.

Grade Level	First and second grades
Costume	Black pants and black top
	Red umbrella with black spots (to use as the shell of the ladybug)
Props	Stuffed ladybug
	Large cardboard clock with movable hands

Other Resources

Web sites

www.ericcarle.com

Videos

Eric Carle: Picture Writer. New York: Philomel Books and Scholastic, Inc., 1993.

Books by Eric Carle

The Very Lonely Firefly

Dream Snow

Hello, Red Fox

The Mixed-up Chameleon

The Very Quiet Cricket

The Very Busy Spider

From Head to Toe

Lesson

Step 1: Read and share the book with the class.

Step 2: Have students sit in a circle. Have one student hold the clock, retell the events on one page, and inform the class of the time. Pass around the clock and let students move the hands to match the pages of the book, describing what happened at each point.

Example: At 5 o'clock the ladybug _____

The time changes 17 times in the story. This will allow many of the students to have a turn. If more jobs are needed to involve more students, here are a few more ideas:

1. A student will rotate around the outside of the circle, carrying the ladybug. This student can let the ladybug pick the next storyteller.

2. Two students can turn the pages of the book.

These two jobs can be changed as needed to ensure that all students get to have a part.

Closure

Ask students to think about the attitude of the ladybug at the beginning and the end of the story. Did she change?

Teacher's Notes:

LESSON 2

Language Arts National Standards

NL-ENG.K-12.3 Evaluation Strategies

Students apply a wide range of strategies to comprehend, interpret, evaluate, and appreciate texts. They draw on their prior experience, their interactions with other readers and writers, their knowledge of word meaning and of other texts, their word identification strategies, and their understanding of textual features (e.g., sound-letter correspondence, sentence structure, context, graphics).

NL-ENG.K-12.4 Communication Skills

Students adjust their use of spoken, written, and visual language (e.g., conventions, style, and vocabulary) to communicate effectively with a variety of audiences and for different purposes.

NL-ENG.K-12.5 Communication Strategies

Students employ a wide range of strategies as they write and use different writing process elements appropriately to communicate with different audiences for a variety of purposes.

NL-ENG.K-12.12 Applying Language Skills

Students use spoken, written, and visual language to accomplish their own purposes (e.g., for learning, enjoyment, persuasion, and the exchange of information).

Skills	Dictionary usage Creative writing

Objective

Students will be able to work in small groups to make an acrostic using the insects in Eric Carle's books.

Grade Level	Second grade

Materials	Collection of Eric Carle books Student and picture dictionaries Words for each group (should be words from the book you have selected, e.g., *cricket, caterpillar, firefly, spider*) Picture of Eric Carle (can be printed from his Web site) White drawing paper (three sheets per group) Scrap paper for rough drafts

Lesson

Step 1: Using the transparency of the Eric Carle acrostic, point out some basic information about this author. Share the picture of Eric Carle and point out the books that are in the library. Point out where the books are located in the library. Reinforce the call number of the Eric Carle books.

Step 2: Divide students into small groups.

Step 3: Explain the acrostic transparency as a form of writing about a person or thing. Point out that each group will be doing an insect acrostic that appears in one of the Eric Carle books. Use the ladybug acrostic to explain that each letter of the word has an adjective or descriptive phrase that helps to identify the insect.

Step 4: If necessary, take one of the books and model another acrostic example on the board. Point out that some words can be found in the book or students can look in the dictionaries.

Step 5: Review with the kids how to use the dictionary.

- ABC order
- Guide words at the tops of pages

Step 6: Give out the Eric Carle books. The students in each group should take turns reading the book first. It might be important to have a strong reader in each group.

Step 7: Give out the paper supplies, insect names, and dictionaries.

Each group should create an acrostic, a picture of the insect, and an illustrated book jacket. It might be helpful to move around the room and assign letters to members of the different groups. The process will move faster if they have a letter to find a word for. The scrap paper can be used to practice on before making the final copy.

Closure

Move into a circle and share what the groups have done. Display the acrostics or put them in a notebook for students to enjoy.

Teacher's Notes:

Transparency
Eric Carle Acrostic

E   Enormously entertaining

R   Relaxed reading

I   Interesting illustrator

C   Creator of the hungry caterpillar

C   Collage—collection of tissue paper pictures

A   Awesome author

R   Radically simple designs

L   Loved by children everywhere

E   Everybody/easy section—where we find his books in our library

Eric Carle
Pattern

Transparency
Ladybug Sample Acrostic

L   Lacks manners

A   Aphids are awesome

D   Doesn't share

Y   Yells a lot

B   Bad-tempered

U   Unkind

G   Grouchy

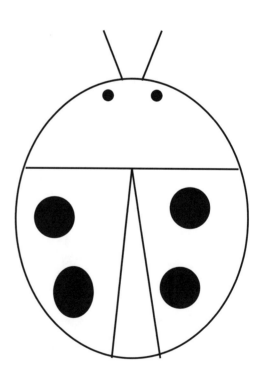

Eric Carle
Extra fun worksheet

Find the words that are hidden in the caterpillar.
Color and add the eyes to make your bug complete.

```
I N S E C T L
V B C R A B N
E U R I R R V
R G A C L A Q
Y S B Z E T R
A P H I D S J
C R I C K E T
R E D I P S E
```

Word Box

• Insect	• Very	• Bugs	• Crab
• Aphids	• Carle	• Eric	• Spider
	• Cricket	• Star	

LESSON 3

Language Arts National Standards

NL-ENG.K-12.1 Reading for Perspective

Students read a wide range of print and nonprint texts to build an understanding of texts, of themselves, and of the cultures of the United States and the world; to acquire new information; to respond to the needs and demands of society and the workplace; and for personal fulfillment. Among these texts are fiction and nonfiction, classic and contemporary works.

NL-ENG.K-12.3 Evaluation Strategies

Students apply a wide range of strategies to comprehend, interpret, evaluate, and appreciate texts. They draw on their prior experience, their interactions with other readers and writers, their knowledge of word meaning and of other texts, their word identification strategies, and their understanding of textual features (e.g., sound-letter correspondence, sentence structure, context, graphics).

NL-ENG.K-12.12 Applying Language Skills

Students use spoken, written, and visual language to accomplish their own purposes (e.g., for learning, enjoyment, persuasion, and the exchange of information).

Skills   Comprehension
             Story elements

Objective

Students will be able to answer questions while playing the game.

Grade Level   Kindergarten and first grade

Materials   Two large dice from a party supply store
               Two caterpillars or butterflies for markers
               Optional: Gummy worms for a treat after the game

Instructions

Enlarge the pattern of the caterpillar onto poster board or fabric. Using markers or paint, add color to the game board. Cut out circles of yellow or green construction paper and write questions on them. Laminate them for longer use. These are the cards for the game.

Make three cards for each of the following and mix in with the other cards.

- Skip a turn

- Go ahead two spaces

- Go back two space

Lesson

Step 1: Introduce the book and author. Read the story aloud and talk about it. Let students share their comments.

Step 2: Play the Caterpillar Game. Divide the class into two teams. Place the game board in the middle of the floor and have students sit along the sides of the board. Students will roll the dice and move a marker, draw a question, and answer the question. Reward the class with gummy worms.

Questions Labeled with Bloom's Levels of Thinking Taxonomy

Knowledge

1. What did the caterpillar turn into?
2. What was one thing the caterpillar ate on Saturday?
3. What did the caterpillar make on Sunday?
4. What was one thing the caterpillar ate on Monday?
5. How long did the caterpillar stay in the cocoon?
6. What was the first thing the caterpillar ate?
7. What did the caterpillar eat on Sunday?
8. How did the caterpillar feel at the end of the day on Saturday?
9. What was the caterpillar's first problem?
10. What did the caterpillar eat on Thursday?
11. What did the caterpillar eat on Friday?
12. How many things did the caterpillar eat on Tuesday?
13. What was the caterpillar's size on Sunday? Fat or big
14. How many things did the caterpillar eat on Wednesday?
15. What did the caterpillar eat on Wednesday?
16. How many things did the caterpillar eat on Thursday?
17. What day did the caterpillar eat pears?
18. How many things were eaten on Friday?
19. How many things did the caterpillar eat on Saturday?

Comprehension

1. Describe the problem in the story.
2. Describe the solution in the story.
3. What foods were vegetables in the story?
4. What foods were junk foods?

Analysis

1. What was your favorite part of the story?
2. What was your favorite illustration in the story?

Teacher's Notes:

The Very Hungry Caterpillar
by Eric Carle
Pattern

32
David Shannon Study: *David Goes to School*

By David Shannon

From David Shannon. *David Goes to School.* New York: Blue Sky Press, 1999.

Language Arts National Standards

NL-ENG.K-12.1 Reading for Perspective

Students read a wide range of print and nonprint texts to build an understanding of texts, of themselves, and of the cultures of the United States and the world; to acquire new information; to respond to the needs and demands of society and the workplace; and for personal fulfillment. Among these texts are fiction and nonfiction, classic and contemporary works.

NL-ENG.K-12.3 Evaluation Strategies

Students apply a wide range of strategies to comprehend, interpret, evaluate, and appreciate texts. They draw on their prior experience, their interactions with other readers and writers, their knowledge of word meaning and of other texts, their word identification strategies, and their understanding of textual features (e.g., sound-letter correspondence, sentence structure, context, graphics).

NL-ENG.K-12.12 Applying Language Skills

Students use spoken, written, and visual language to accomplish their own purposes (e.g., for learning, enjoyment, persuasion, and the exchange of information).

Skills
Author study
Retelling—younger students
Creative writing—older students

Objective

Students will become familiar with the author, David Shannon. Younger students will retell the story using the props in the canvas bag. Older students will write a class story about another adventure with David.

Grade Level   Kindergarten through second grade

Props   Laminated school late pass with David's name on it
Chalk and eraser
Bubble gum
Laminated pair of hands cut from construction paper
Jar of paint
Clouds made of cotton balls on a blue piece of construction paper
Lunch box

Ball
Small books and pencils
Restroom pass (piece of laminated paper with "Restroom Pass" written on
        it and a string attached)
Box of crayons
Small sponge and small bucket
Large gold star
Canvas bag with "David" written on the side in puffy paint

Materials   Chart paper or dry eraser board
Lined paper
Pencils and crayons
Cotton balls
One piece of blue-and-white construction paper
Yarn or string
Gold wrapping paper
Tag board
Rubber cement and scissors
Puffy paint

Instructions: Prelesson Preparation

Cut a star from wrapping paper and tag board. Rubber cement the wrapping paper to the tag board and laminate it.

Gather information about David Shannon from the inside back flap of his books or the Scholastic Press Web site, www.scholastic.com. Using the pattern with "David Shannon" and the clouds of thoughts on it, write the facts on the clouds and laminate the paper. Enlarge the picture of "David" onto a large piece of paper and laminate it.

Lesson

Step 1: Introduce the author, David Shannon. While sharing facts about David Shannon, place the clouds on the enlarged picture of David.

Step 2: Introduce the book and read the story *David Goes to School.*

Step 3: Show kindergarten and first grade students the canvas bag of props. Draw a few out and ask if they remember when in the story the item was used. Select students to retell the story. Give the selected students the props and have them retell the story to the class. Select more students until all have had a turn to help retell the story.

Step 4: Another idea for the younger students is to read *No, David* and illustrate a class book about "Yes, David." Brainstorm ideas and let students create a page using the worksheet for "Yes, David."

Step 5: Older students will brainstorm ideas for a class story about another adventure with David. Using the dry eraser board, write down the students' ideas for the title of the class story.

Examples: "David Goes to the Grocery Story," "David Goes to the Mall," or "David Goes to the Movies." The class will agree on the title for a class story. Each student will create a page for the class story. Laminate and bind the pages into a book and display it in the library for other classes to read.

David Shannon was born in
Washington, D.C.

Cloud Example for Facts

David Goes to School
by David Shannon
Pattern

No, David
by David Shannon
Worksheet

Yes, David

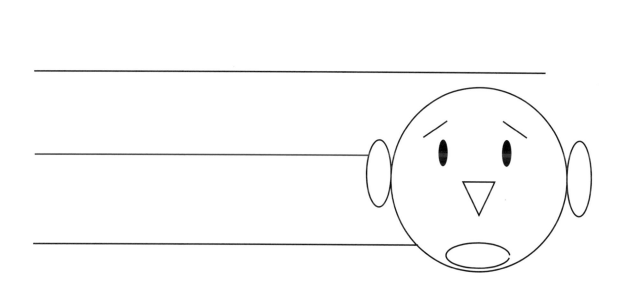

33
Jan Brett Study: *The Mitten* and *The Hat*

From Jan Brett. *The Mitten*. New York: Putnam, 1989 (lesson 2).
From Jan Brett. *The Hat*. New York: Putnam, 1997 (lesson 3).

LESSON 1: AUTHOR STUDY

Language Arts National Standards

NL-ENG.K-12.7 Evaluating Data

Students conduct research on issues and interests by generating ideas and questions and by posing problems. They gather, evaluate, and synthesize data from a variety of sources to communicate their discoveries in ways that suit their purpose and audience.

NL-ENG.K-12.8 Developing Research Skills

Students use a variety of technological and information resources to gather and synthesize information and to create and communicate knowledge.

NL-ENG.K-12.11 Participating in Society

Students participate as knowledgeable, reflective, creative, and critical members of a variety of literacy communities.

NL-ENG.K-12.12 Applying Language Skills

Students use spoken, written, and visual language to accomplish their own purposes (e.g., for learning, enjoyment, persuasion, and the exchange of information).

Skills   Timeline
               Author study
               Research

Objective

Students will become familiar with the author, Jan Brett. Students will also research facts and place them on the timeline.

Grade Level   First and second grades

Materials   Sentence strips
                  Black marker
                  Red construction paper
                  Cotton balls

Instructions

1. Make 10 or 12 red hats using the pattern and glue cotton balls on the top of the hat for a pom-pom.

2. Prepare sentence strips with the timeline.

-1949----------1950--

Timeline Example

3. Find date facts about Jan Brett on her Web site. *Example:* She was born in 1949. Her first book, *Fritz and the Beautiful Horses,* was written in 1981. Write facts on the red hats. Tape the timeline up around the room on shelves or walls.

Resources

Web sites

www.janbrett.com

Books

Kovags, Deborah. *Meet the Authors and Illustrators: Volume Two.* New York: Scholastic, 1993.

Something About the Author, Volume 130. Detroit: Thomson Gale, 2002, pp. 22–28.

Any other author sources that are available

Lesson: Author Study

Step 1: Introduce the author, Jan Brett. Show the timeline, which has been tacked up around the room, and talk about important dates in the students' lives. *Examples:* "What year were you born? What year is it now?" Tell students that they are going to learn important dates in Jan Brett's life. Use the hats with the facts and tell younger students about Jan Brett. Older students will research Jan Brett on her Web site. Divide the class into two groups. One group can search for facts on the computer and the other group can search using printed sources. Encourage students to find facts with dates. Students can work in pairs. After allowing students to research, gather the class together and share the facts. Write the facts on the board and select students to transfer them to the red hats.

Step 2: Students will place the facts on the timeline in the appropriate dates. Mix the hats and have the students place them on the timeline.

Teacher's Notes:

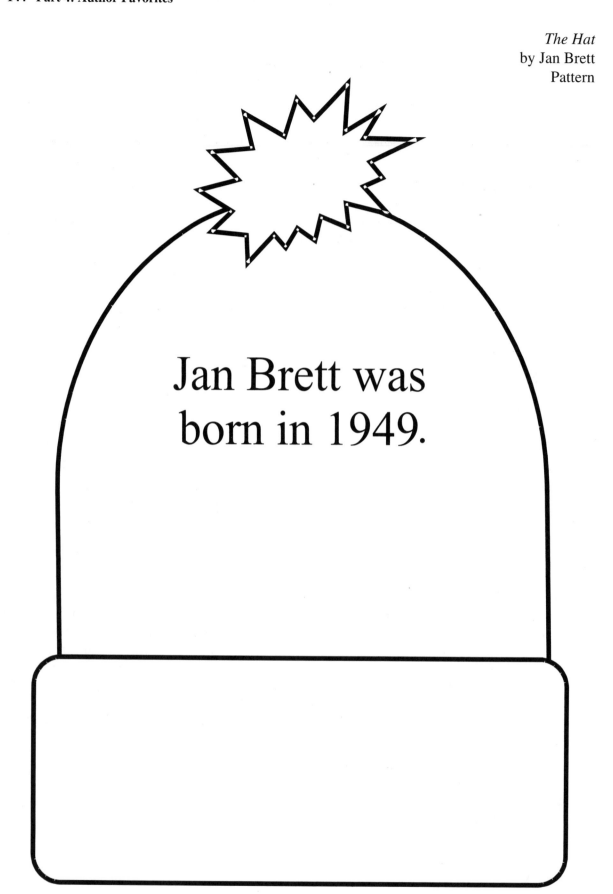

Jan Brett was
born in 1949.

LESSON 2: *THE MITTEN*

Language Arts National Standards

NL-ENG.K12.1 Reading for Perspective

Students read a wide range of print and nonprint texts to build an understanding of texts, of themselves, and of the culture of the United States and the world; to acquire new information; to respond to the needs and the demands of society and the workplace; and for personal fulfillment. Among these texts are fiction and nonfiction, classic and contemporary works.

NL-ENG.K12.3 Evaluation Strategies

Students apply a wide range of strategies to comprehend, interpret, evaluate, and appreciate texts. They draw on their prior experience, their interactions with other readers and writers, their knowledge of word meaning and of other texts, their word identification strategies, and their understanding of textual features (e.g., sound-letter correspondence, sentence structure, context, graphics).

Skills	Retelling Sequencing

Objective

Students will be able to recall the order that the animals appeared in the story.

Grade Level	First and second grades
Costume	Winter scarf and hat
Props	Small stuffed owl, badger, mole, bear, fox, hedgehog, rabbit, and a mouse (if it is difficult to find these animals, use pictures of animals or a generic animal with the name hedgehog on it). Assortment of stuffed animals for the reading station
Materials	White stretch knit fabric Coloring pages from the Jan Brett Web site Collection of books by the author Winter theme stickers

Instructions

Enlarge the mitten pattern, cut two from the fabric, and stitch them together, leaving an opening for the animals.

Lesson

Step 1: Seat students in the story corner. As you put on the winter hat and scarf, introduce the book and author. Show the book and stress where these books are located in the library.

Step 2: Tell the story using the mitten. As each animal appears and climbs into the mitten, have animals ready and place them inside. Practice ahead of time so that the mitten is stretched enough and you are familiar with the events of the story.

Step 3: Line up all of the animals and ask students to arrange them in the order that they appear in the story.

Closure

Set up stations around the room. Give each station a number for easier flow. Count off students and assign them to the stations. Eight to six students can be in each group. Switch stations as time allows or leave them set up and carry them over to another class period. Give out stickers as students complete each station.

Stations

1. Retelling the story. Leave the stuffed animals and mitten out so that students can act out the story.

2. Coloring pages and crayons

3. Reading center. Students pick a book and read to a stuffed animal.

4. Drawing: Run off copies of the mitten. Students can draw all of the animals inside the mitten.

Teacher's Notes:

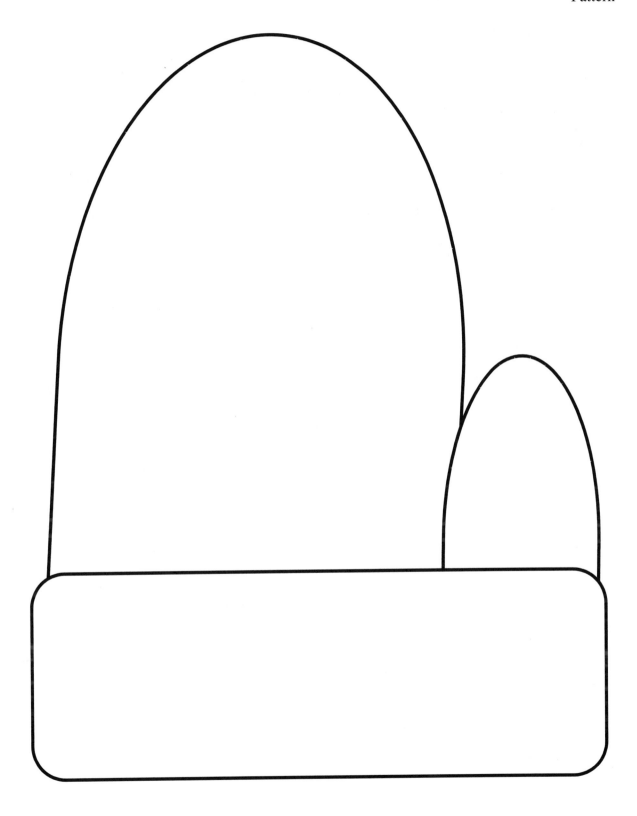

LESSON 3: *THE HAT*

Language Arts National Standards

NL-ENG.K-12.1 Reading for Perspective

Students read a wide range of print and nonprint texts to build an understanding of texts, of themselves, and of the cultures of the United States and the world; to acquire new information; to respond to the needs and demands of society and the workplace; and for personal fulfillment. Among these texts are fiction and nonfiction, classic and contemporary works.

NL-ENG.K-12.3 Evaluation Strategies

Students apply a wide range of strategies to comprehend, interpret, evaluate, and appreciate texts. They draw on their prior experience, their interactions with other readers and writers, their knowledge of word meaning and of other texts, their word identification strategies, and their understanding of textual features (e.g., sound-letter correspondence, sentence structure, context, graphics).

Skills   Retelling

Objective

Students will be able to retell the story using the puppets and story lines.

Grade Level   First and second grades

Materials   Puppets from Jan Brett's Web site
Tag board
Rubber cement
Construction paper
Yarn for a clothesline
Clothes pins

Instructions: Preparing the Materials

Print puppets from the Web site. Glue puppets to tag board, cut them out, and laminate them. Type phrases from the story on regular size paper and back it with construction paper, then laminate. String the clothesline across the library and place clothes pins on the line.

Examples of phrases

Lisa took her woolen clothes outside.

She hung her clothes on the line and the wind took one of her stockings.

Hedgie found the stocking and put his head in the opening and it stuck to his prickles.

Resources

Web sites

www.janbrett.com

Lesson

Step 1: Introduce the book and author. Tell students to pay attention to the illustrations; they are very important to the story. Read the story and discuss the illustrations.

Step 2: Pass out the puppets and dialog. Hopefully there are enough puppets and phrases from the story for everyone to have one.

Step 3: Students will put the story in order using the puppets and phrases, then hang them on the clothesline across the library.

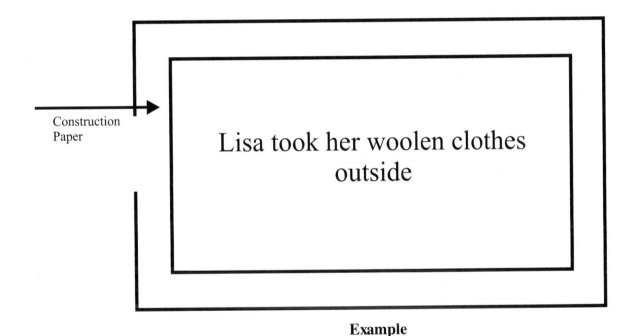

Construction Paper

Lisa took her woolen clothes outside

Example

Teacher's Notes:

34
Louise Borden Study: *A. Lincoln and Me*

By Louise Borden

From Louise Borden. *A. Lincoln and Me*. New York: Scholastic Press, 1999.

Language Arts National Standards

NL-ENG.K-12.1 Reading for Perspective

Students read a wide range of print and nonprint texts to build an understanding of texts, of themselves, and of the cultures of the United States and the world; to acquire new information; to respond to the needs and demands of society and the workplace; and for personal fulfillment. Among these texts are fiction and nonfiction, classic and contemporary works.

NL-ENG.K-12.7 Evaluating Data

Students conduct research on issues and interests by generating ideas and questions and by posing problems. They gather, evaluate, and synthesize data from a variety of sources to communicate their discoveries in ways that suit their purpose and audience.

NL-ENG.K-12.8 Developing Research Skills

Students use a variety of technological and information resources to gather and synthesize information and to create and communicate knowledge.

NL-ENG.K-12.11 Participating in Society

Students participate as knowledgeable, reflective, creative, and critical members of a variety of literacy communities.

NL-ENG.K-12.12 Applying Language Skills

Students use spoken, written, and visual language to accomplish their own purposes (e.g., for learning, enjoyment, persuasion, and the exchange of information).

Skills   Author study
            Illustrating
            Older students: Research skills on the Internet and other resources

Objective

Students will become familiar with the author, Louise Borden, and the sixteenth president, Abraham Lincoln. Students will write words to describe themselves and draw a picture of themselves. Older students will practice collecting data from a Web site and other resources.

Grade Level   First and second grades

Materials   Tape measure
Scales to weigh students
Chart paper or wipe-off board
Markers
Tag board for hat pattern

Instructions

Enlarge the hat pattern on chart paper to fit an easel or dry eraser board. This will be used to display facts about Louise Borden and Abraham Lincoln. Cut out the hats and write facts about the author on the smaller hats. Make a large and a small pattern out of tag board for students to trace.

Props   Large black top hat (from a party supply store) to use as the storage medium for facts about the author

Resources

Web sites

www.louiseborden.com

Videos

Abraham Lincoln. Washington, DC: Atlas Video, 1990.

Books

Adler, David A. *A Picture Book of Abraham Lincoln.* New York: Holiday House, 1989.

Armentrout, David. *Abraham Lincoln.* Vero Beach, Fla.: Rourke Publishing, 2002.

Lesson

Step 1: Introduce the author, Louise Borden, by showing some books she has written. Make a display of books in an area where students can see them easily. Students will share facts by drawing the facts out of the large black hat. Display the facts on the enlarged hat. Older students may research Louise Borden by visiting her Web site. Students may also research Abraham Lincoln. Older students may work in pairs, write down one fact about Louise Borden or Abraham Lincoln, and share it with the class.

Step 2: Read the book and talk about Abraham Lincoln. Recall facts about Lincoln from the book. Write the facts on chart paper or the wipe-off board. Students can share writing the facts.

Step 3: Reread the last page and talk about how special and different everyone is and that there is only one of everyone.

Step 4: Weigh and measure the students.

Step 5: Activity:

1. Make copies of large black hat pattern on tag board.

2. Students will trace and cut out a large black hat(see the pattern).

3. Students will complete the worksheet by filling in the blanks and drawing a picture of themselves. An option for this activity is to take pictures of students with a digital camera. Print, cut out, and glue them on the worksheet.

4. Students will cut out the worksheet and glue it on the black hat.

5. Display the finished hats in the classroom or library.

Teacher's Notes:

A. Lincoln and Me
by Louise Borden
Large Black Hat Pattern

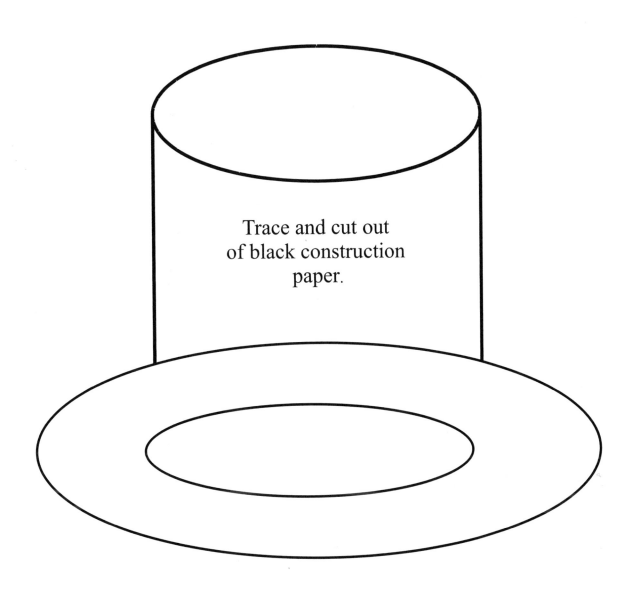

Trace and cut out
of black construction
paper.

I have _____ hair.

I have _____ eyes.

I am _____ inches tall.

I am _____ years old.

Nobody can be another me.

Complete the sentences. Draw a picture of yourself in the large oval.
Cut it out and glue it into the black hat.

35

Mike Thaler Study:
The Librarian from the Black Lagoon

By Mike Thaler

From Mike Thaler. *The Librarian from the Black Lagoon.* New York: Scholastic, 1997.

Language Arts National Standards

NL-ENG.K-12.7 Evaluating Data

Students conduct research on issues and interests by generating ideas and questions and by posing problems. They gather, evaluate, and synthesize data from a variety of sources to communicate their discoveries in ways that suit their purpose and audience.

NL-ENG.K-12.8 Developing Research Skills

Students use a variety of technological and information resources to gather and synthesize information and to create and communicate knowledge.

NL-ENG.K-12.11 Participating in Society

Students participate as knowledgeable, reflective, creative, and critical members of a variety of literacy communities.

Skills   Author study

Objective

Students will become familiar with the author, Mike Thaler. Older students will research several sources and share facts with the class. Students will also create and name a student from the Black Lagoon.

Grade Level   First and second grades

Props   A life-size cardboard cutout of a body
Clothes and shoes for the body

Materials   Laminated facts about the author on construction paper (see Web site)
Paper plates
Small outline of body (see pattern) for each student
Crayons and pencils
Various colors of construction paper for hair
Books written by the author
A picture of the author's face printed from the Internet

Resources

Web sites

www.mikethaler.com

Books

Thaler, Mike. *Imagination.* Katonah, N.Y.: Richard C. Owen, 2002.

Something About the Author, Volume 93. Detroit: Gale, 1997, pp. 196–201.

Any other resources that would be available.

Lesson

Step 1: Introduce author Mike Thaler using the cardboard cutout and facts. Display facts on the cutout in the folds of the clothes, pockets, belt, etc. Older students can research Mike Thaler using the listed resources and share what they find with the class. Divide the class into pairs and let them work together to find facts. The students may share their facts by placing them on the cardboard body.

Step 2: Show books written by Mike Thaler.

Step 3: Read *The Librarian from the Black Lagoon.* Discuss the story and pictures. Talk about how Mike Thaler makes his characters weird and ugly.

Step 4: Using the outline of the body and paper plate, students will make a student from the Black Lagoon. The paper plate will be the head. Add construction paper for the hair. After completing the student, the class will name it. Because Mike Thaler is America's Riddle King, students should use a two-word name that rhymes or have both parts of the name start the same. *Examples:* Pretty Patty, Lucky Luke, or Bill the Pill. Students will record their student's name on a piece of paper.

Step 5: Staple the name to the student and display it in the classroom or media center.

Other Books by Mike Thaler

The Teacher from the Black Lagoon

The School Nurse from the Black Lagoon

The Music Teacher from the Black Lagoon

The Principal from the Black Lagoon

The Gym Teacher from the Black Lagoon

The Cafeteria Lady from the Black Lagoon

The Custodian from the Black Lagoon

The Class from the Black Lagoon

Teacher's Notes:

The Librarian from the Black Lagoon
by Mike Thaler
Pattern

Appendix

NL-ENG.K-12.1 Reading for Perspective

A. Lincoln and Me
Bark, George
Alligator Baby
Cindy Ellen: A Wild Western Cinderella
Cobweb Christmas
David Goes to School
The Grouchy Ladybug
The Napping House
The Jacket I Wear in the Snow
Joseph Had a Little Overcoat
The Little Red Hen (Makes a Pizza)
Miss Spider's Tea Party
Strega Nona Takes a Vacation
The Very Hungry Caterpillar
When Winter Comes

NL-ENG.K-12.2 Understanding the Human Experience

Alligator Baby
Cindy Ellen: A Wild Western Cinderella
The Jacket I Wear in the Snow
The Little Red Hen (Makes a Pizza)

NL-ENG.K-12.3 Evaluation Strategies

Alligator Baby
The Bag I'm Taking to Grandma's
Bark, George
Big Al
Cobweb Christmas
David Goes to School
D.W. the Picky Eater
Franklin's Halloween
The Frog Principal
Grandpa's Teeth
The Grouchy Ladybug
The Jacket I Wear in the Snow
Joseph Had a Little Overcoat
The Lady with the Alligator Purse
Maxwell's Magic Mix-Up

Mrs. Piccolo's Easy Chair
The Napping House
Rabbit Food
The Rainbow Fish
Show and Tell Bunnies
Strega Nona Takes a Vacation
The Teeny Tiny Teacher
Timothy Goes to School
The Very Hungry Caterpillar
Welcome Back to Pokeweed Public School

NL-ENG.K-12.4 Communication Skills

The Big Green Pocketbook
The Frog Principal
If You Take a Mouse to the Movies
Is Your Mama a Llama?
The Teeny Tiny Teacher

NL-ENG.K-12.5 Communication Strategies

The Big Green Pocketbook
The Frog Principal
If You Take a Mouse to the Movies
Is Your Mama a Llama?
The Rainbow Fish
The Teeny Tiny Teacher
Timothy Goes to School

NL-ENG.K-12.7 Evaluating Data

A. Lincoln and Me
Bark, George
The Hat
The Librarian from the Black Lagoon
The Mitten
Show and Tell Bunnies

NL-ENG.K-12.8 Developing Research Skills

A. Lincoln and Me
The Hat
The Librarian from the Black Lagoon
The Mitten

NL-ENG.K-12.11 Participating in Society

A. Lincoln and Me
Alligator Baby
The Bag I'm Taking to Grandma's
Big Al
Cobweb Christmas
D.W. the Picky Eater
Grandpa's Teeth
The Hat
The Jacket I Wear in the Snow
The Lady with the Alligator Purse
The Librarian from the Black Lagoon
Maxwell's Magic Mix-Up
The Mitten
Mrs. Piccolo's Easy Chair
Strega Nona Takes a Vacation
The Teeny Tiny Teacher
'Twas the Night Before Thanksgiving
When Winter Comes

NL-ENG.K-12.12 Applying Language Skills

A. Lincoln and Me
Cindy Ellen: A Wild Western Cinderella
David Goes to School
Franklin's Halloween
The Frog Principal
The Hat
The Librarian from the Black Lagoon
The Little Red Hen (Makes a Pizza)
Miss Spider's Tea Party
The Mitten
The Rainbow Fish
Show and Tell Bunnies
Timothy Goes to School
The Very Hungry Caterpillar
'Twas the Night Before Thanksgiving

Web Resources

John Bianchi	www.bunglobooks.com
Louise Borden	www.louiseborden.com
Marc Brown	www.pbskids.org/arthur/
Jan Brett	www.janbrett.com
Eric Carle	www.eric-carle.com
Tomie dePaola	www.bingley.com
Learning Skills Program	www.coun.uvic.ca/learn/program/hndouts/bloom.html
Robert Munsch	www.robertmunsch.com
National Council of Teachers of English	www.ncte.org
Laura Numeroff	www.lauranumeroff.com
Mike Thaler	www.mikethaler.com
Audrey Wood and Don Wood	www.audreywood.com
Scholastic	www.scholastic.com

Bibliography

Ashman, Linda. *Maxwell's Magic Mix-up*. New York: Simon & Schuster Books for Young Readers, 2001.

Bianchi, John. *Welcome Back to Pokeweed Public School*. Buffalo, N.Y.: Bungalo Books, 1996.

Bloom, Benjamin. *Taxonomy of Educational Objectives: Handbook 1, The Cognitive Domain*. New York: David McKay, 1956.

Borden, Louise. *A. Lincoln and Me*. New York: Scholastic, 1999.

Bourgeois, Paulette. *Franklin's Halloween*. New York: Scholastic, 1996.

Brett, Jan. *The Hat*. New York: Putnam, 1997.

———. *The Mitten*. New York: Putnam, 1989.

Brown, Marc. *D.W., the Picky Eater*. Boston: Little, Brown, 1995.

Calmenson, Stephanie. *The Frog Principal*. New York: Scholastic, 2001.

———. *The Teeny Tiny Teacher*. New York: Scholastic , 1998.

Carle, Eric. *The Grouchy Ladybug*. New York: HarperCollins, 1996.

———. *The Very Hungry Caterpillar*. New York: Collins, 1979.

Clement, Rod. *Grandpa's Teeth*. Sydney, Australia: HarperCollins, 1997.

Clements, Andrew. *Big Al*. New York: Simon & Schuster Books for Young Readers, 188.

Climo, Shirley. *Cobweb Christmas*. New York: HarperCollins, 2001.

dePaola, Tomie. *Strega Nona Takes a Vacation*. New York: Putnam, 2000.

Feiffer, Jules. *Bark, George*. New York: HarperCollins, 1999.

Galdone, Paul. *The Little Red Hen*. New York: Seaburg, 1973.

Gretz, Susanna. *Rabbit Food*. Cambridge, Mass.: Candlewick Press, 1999.

Guarino, Deborah. *Is Your Mama a Llama?* New York: Scholastic., 1989.

Jackson, Jean. *Mrs. Piccolo's Easy Chair*. New York: DK Publishing, 1999.

Kirk, David. *Miss Spider's Tea Party*. New York: Scholastic, 1994.

Lasky, Kathryn. *Show and Tell Bunnies*. Cambridge, Mass.: Candlewick Press, 1998.

Lowell, Susan. *Cindy Ellen: A Wild Western Cinderella*. New York: HarperCollins, 2000.

Moore, Clement C. *The Night Before Christmas*. Philadelphia: Running Press, 1995.

Munsch, Robert. *Alligator Baby*. New York: Scholastic, 1997.

National Council of Teachers of English and International Reading Association. *Standards for the English Language Arts*. Urbana, IL: NCTE, 1996.

Neitzel, Shirley. *The Bag I'm Taking to Grandma's*. New York: Scholastic, 1995.

———. *The Jacket I Wear in the Snow*. New York: Greenwillow Books, 1989.

Numeroff, Laura. *If You Take a Mouse to the Movies*. New York: HarperCollins, 2000.

Pfister, Marcus. *The Rainbow Fish*. New York: North South Books, 1992.

Pilkey, Dav. *'Twas the Night Before Thanksgiving*. New York: Scholastic, 1990.

Ransom, Candice. *The Big Green Pocketbook*. New York: HarperCollins, 1993.

Shannon, David. *David Goes to School*. New York: Blue Sky Press, 1999.

Sturges, Philemon. *The Little Red Hen (Makes a Pizza)*. New York: Dutton Children's Books, 1999.

Taback, Simms. *Joseph Had a Little Overcoat*. New York: Viking Press, 1999.

Thaler, Mike. *The Librarian from the Black Lagoon*. New York: Scholastic, 1997.

Van Laan, Nancy. *When Winter Comes*. New York: Atheneum Books for Young Readers, 2000.

Wells, Rosemary. *Timothy Goes to School*. New York: Penguin Group, 2000.

Westcott, Nadine Bernard. *The Lady with the Alligator Purse*. Boston: Little, Brown, 1988.

Wood, Audrey. *The Napping House*. San Diego: Harcourt Brace Jovanovich, 1984.

Index

A. Lincoln and Me activities, 150–154
  language arts standards, 150
  pattern, 153
  skills, 150
  worksheet, 150
Abraham Lincoln, 151
Activities. *See also* Kindergarten activities;
    First-grade activities; Second-grade
    activities
  about authors, 125–157
  for *Alligator Baby,* 26–28
  for *Bag I'm Taking to Grandma's,* 63–65
  for *Bark, George,* 79–81
  for *Big Al,* 82–85
  for *Big Green Pocketbook,* 3–5
  for *Cindy Ellen,* 86–88
  for *Cobweb Christmas,* 53–56
  for David Shannon, 137–141
  for *D.W. the Picky Eater,* 60
  for Eric Carle, 127–136
  for *Franklin's Halloween,* 50–52
  for *Frog Principal,* 41–45
  for *Grandpa's Teeth,* 96–99
  for *If You Take a Mouse to the Movies,* 29–33
  involving comprehension, 39–75
  involving retelling, 1–38
  involving story elements, 77–123
  for *Is Your Mama a Llama?,* 34–38
  for *Jacket I Wear in the Snow,* 23–25
  for Jan Brett,142–149
  for *Joseph Had a Little Overcoat,* 9–12
  for *Lady with the Alligator Purse,* 89–95
  for *Little Red Hen,* 100–102
  for Louise Borden, 150–154
  for *Maxwell's Magic Mix-Up,* 46–49
  for Mike Thaler, 155–157
  for *Miss Spider's Tea Party,* 103–106
  for *Mrs. Piccolo's Easy Chair,* 59
  for *Napping House,* 6–8
  for *Rabbit Food,* 16–18
  for *Rainbow Fish,* 69–72
  for *Show and Tell Bunnies,* 117–123
  for *Strega Nona Takes a Vacation,* 66–68
  for *Teeny Tiny Teacher,* 19–22
  for *Timothy Goes to School,* 73–75
  for *'Twas the Night Before Thanksgiving,*
    107–114
  for *Welcome Back to Pokewood Public
    School,* 13–15
  for *When Winter Comes,* 115–116
Adler, David A., 151
Alligator Baby activities, 26–28
  language arts standards, 26
  skills, 26
  worksheet, 28
Applying language skills, xi, 41, 50, 69, 73, 86,
    100, 103, 107, 117, 129, 134, 137, 142,
    150
Armentrout, David, 151
Ashman, Linda, 46–49
Author-focused activities, 125–157

Bag I'm Taking to Grandma's activities, 63–65
  language arts standards, 63
  skills, 63
  worksheet, 65
Bark, George activities, 79–81
  language arts standards, 79
  skills, 79
  worksheet, 81
Bianchi, John, 13–15
Big Al activities, 82–85
  language arts standards, 82
  skills, 82
  summary chart, 85
  worksheet, 84
Big Green Pocketbook activities, 3–4
  language arts standards, 3
  skills, 3
Bloom's Taxonomy, questions using
  analysis, 58, 71, 74, 97, 98, 135
  application, 43, 51, 54, 67, 71, 74, 97, 98
  comprehension, 14, 43, 51, 54, 58, 67, 70, 74,
    97, 98, 135
  evaluation, 71
  knowledge, 42, 51, 54, 58, 67, 70, 74, 97, 98,
    135
  synthesis, 43, 58, 71
Borden, Louise, 150–154
Bourgeois, Paulette, 50–52
Brett, Jan, 142–149
Brown, Marc, 60–62

Cafeteria Lady from the Black Lagoon (Thaler), 156
Calmenson, Stephanie, 19–22, 41–45
Carle, Eric, 127–136
Cindy Ellen: A Wild Western Cinderella
    activities, 86–88
    language arts standards, 86
    skills, 86
    worksheet, 88
Class from the Black Lagoon (Thaler), 156
Clement, Rod, 96–99
Clements, Andrew, 82–85
Climo, Shirley, 53–56
Cobweb Christmas activities, 53–56
    language arts standards, 53
    patterns, 55–56
    skills, 53
Communication skills, xi, 3, 19, 29, 41, 129
Communication strategies, xi, 3, 19, 29, 41, 69,
    73, 129
Comprehension activities, 14, 39–75
Custodian from the Black Lagoon (Thaler), 156

D.W. the Picky Eater activities, 60–62
    language arts standards, 60
    skills, 60
    worksheet, 62
David Goes to School activities, 137–141
    language arts standards, 137
    patterns, 139–140
    skills, 137
    worksheet, 141
dePaola, Tomie, 66–68
Developing research skills, xi, 142, 150, 155
Dream Snow (Carle), 128

English language arts standards
    applying language skills, xi, 41, 50, 69, 73,
        86, 100, 103, 107, 117, 129, 134, 137,
        142, 150
    communication skills, xi, 3, 19, 29, 34, 41, 129
    communication strategies, xi, 3, 19, 29, 34,
        41, 69, 73, 129
    developing research skills, xi, 142, 150, 155
    evaluating data, xi, 142, 150, 155
    evaluation strategies, xi, 6, 9, 13, 16, 19, 23,
        26, 41, 46, 50, 53, 57, 60, 63, 66, 69,
        73, 79, 82, 89, 96, 117, 127, 129, 134,
        137, 145
    participating in society, xi, 19, 23, 26, 46, 53,
        57, 60, 63, 66, 82, 89, 96, 107, 115,
        142, 150, 155

    reading for perspective, xi, 6, 9, 23, 26, 53,
        79, 86, 100, 103, 115, 127, 134, 137,
        145, 150
    understanding the human experience, xi, 23,
        26, 86, 100
Eric Carle: Picture Writer, 128
Evaluating data, xi, 142, 150, 155
Evaluation strategies, xi, 6, 9, 13, 16, 19, 23, 26,
    41, 46, 50, 53, 57, 60, 63, 66, 69, 73, 79, 82,
    89, 96, 117, 127, 129, 134, 137, 145, 148

Feiffer, Jules, 79–81
First-grade activities, 9–12, 13–15, 26–28,
    29–33, 41–45, 50–52, 53–56, 57–59,
    60–62, 66–68, 79–81, 82–85, 89–95,
    96–99, 100–102, 103–106, 115–116,
    117–123. 127–128, 134–136, 137–141,
    142–149, 151, 155–157
Franklin's Halloween activities, 50–52
    language arts standards, 50
    pattern, 52
    skills, 50
Frog Principal activities, 41–45
    language arts standards, 41
    pattern, 44
    skills, 41
    worksheet, 45
From Head to Toe (Carle), 128

Grandpa's Teeth activities, 96–99
    language arts standards, 96
    patterns, 97, 99
    skills, 96
Gretz, Susanna, 16–18
Grouchy Ladybug activities, 127–130, 132
    language arts standards, 127, 129
    skills, 127, 129
    transparency, 132
Guarino, Deborah, 34–38
Gym Teacher from the Black Lagoon (Thaler), 156

Hat activities, 148–149
    language arts standards, 148
    pattern, 149
    skills, 148
Hello, Red Fox (Carle), 128

If You Take a Mouse to the Movies activities, 29–33
    language arts standards, 29
    patterns, 32–33
    skills, 29
    worksheet, 31

Imagination (Thaler), 156
Is Your Mama a Llama? activities, 34–38
    language arts standards, 34
    patterns, 37–38
    skills, 34
    worksheet, 36

Jacket I Wear in the Snow activities, 23–25
    language arts standards, 23
    skills, 23
    worksheet, 23
Jackson, Jean, 57–59
Joseph Had a Little Overcoat activities, 9–12
    language arts standards, 9
    skills, 9
    patterns, 11–12

Kindergarten activities, 13–15, 16–18, 41–45,
    57–59, 60–62, 66–68, 73–75, 89–95,
    96–99, 134–136, 137–141
Kirk, David, 103–106

Lady with the Alligator Purse activities, 89–95
    language arts standards, 89
    patterns, 89, 91
    skills, 89
    summary chart, 92
    worksheets, 93–95
Lasky, Kathryn, 117–123
Librarian from the Black Lagoon activities,
    155–157
    language arts standards, 155
    pattern, 157
    skills, 155
Little Red Hen (Makes a Pizza) activities, 100–102
    language arts standards, 100
    overhead, 102
    skills, 100
Lowell, Susan, 86–88

Maxwell's Magic Mix-Up activities, 46–49
    language arts standards, 46
    pattern, 49
    skills, 46
    worksheet, 48
Miss Spider's Tea Party actvities, 103–106
    language arts standards, 103
    skills, 103
    worksheets, 105–106
Mitten activities, 144–147
    language arts standards, 142
    patterns, 144, 147
    skills, 142

Mixed-up Chameleon (Carle), 128
Mrs. Piccolo's Easy Chair activities, 57–59
    language arts skills, 57
    pattern, 59
    skills, 57
Munsch, Robert, 26–28
Music Teacher from the Black Lagoon (Thaler),
    156

Napping House activities, 6–8
    language arts standards, 6
    skills, 6
    worksheet, 8
Neitzel, Shirley, 23–25, 63–65
Numeroff, Laura, 29–33

Participating in society, xi, 19, 23, 26, 46, 53,
    57, 60, 63, 66, 82, 89, 96, 107, 115, 142,
    150, 155
Patterns
    of buildings, 15
    of clothes, 11–12, 44–45, 109, 121, 123
    of a crayon, 74
    for *Cobweb Christmas*, 55–56
    for David Shannon, 139–140
    for Eric Carle, 131–132, 136
    of food, 44–45, 55–56, 111
    of a fort, 32
    for *Franklin's Halloween*, 52
    for *Frog Principal*, 44–45
    of a ghost, 52
    for *Grandpa's Teeth*, 97, 99
    for *If You take a Mouse to the Movies*, 32–33
    for *Is Your Mama a Llama?*, 37–38
    for Jan Brett, 144,147, 149
    for *Joseph Had a Little Overcoat*, 11–12
    of a llama, 37–38
    for Louise Borden, 153–154
    for *Maxwell's Magic Mix-Up*, 49
    for Mike Thaler, 157
    of movie-related items, 33
    for *Mrs. Picccolo's Easy Chair*, 59
    of rabbits, 18, 119–120
    for *Show and Tell Bunnies*, 119–123
    of a snowman, 32
    for *Strega Nona Takes a Vacation*, 68
    of teeth, 97, 99
    of trees, 32, 114
    for *'Twas the Night Before Thanksgiving*,
        108, 109–114
    for *Welcome Back to Pokewood Public
        School,* 15
Pfister, Narcus, 69–72

Picture Book of Abraham Lincoln, 151
Pilkey, Dav, 107–114
Principal from the Black Lagoon (Thaler), 156

Rabbit Food activities, 16–18
    language arts standards, 16
    skills, 16
    pattern, 18
Rainbow Fish activities, 69–72
    language arts standards, 69
    skills, 69
    worksheet, 69
Ransom, Candice, 3–5
Reading for perspective, xi, 6, 9, 23, 26, 53, 79,
    86, 100, 103, 115, 127, 134, 137, 145,
    148, 150
Retelling activities, 1–38

School Nurse from the Black Lagoon (Thaler),
    156
Second-grade activities, 3–5, 6–8, 9–12, 13–15,
    19–22, 23–25, 26–28, 29–33, 34–38,
    41–45, 46–49, 50–52, 53–56, 57–59,
    60–62, 63–65, 66–68, 69–72, 82–85,
    86–88, 89–95, 96–99, 100–102, 103–106,
    107–114, 117–123, 127–130, 137–141,
    142–149, 151, 155–157
Shannon, David, 137–141
Show and Tell Bunnies activities, 117–123
    language arts standards, 117
    patterns, 119–123
    skills, 117
Skills
    author study, 137, 142, 150, 155
    career awareness, 89
    comparing and contrasting, 100, 107
    creating timelines, 142
    creative writing, 3, 23, 41, 50, 129, 137
    dictionary use, 89, 129
    identification of color words, 73
    identifying elements of the story, 79, 82, 86,
        89, 96, 100, 103, 107, 115, 134
    identifying characters, 9, 79, 117
    identifying parts of the library, 96
    illustrating, 150
    oral communication, 26
    problem solving, 117
    reading comprehension, 13, 41, 46, 50, 53,
        57, 60, 63, 66, 69, 73, 134
    research, 142, 150
    retelling, 3, 6, 16, 19, 23, 26, 29, 34, 127,
        137, 145, 148
    sequencing, 6, 9, 13, 29, 145

    shared writing, 19
    telling time, 127
    writing and illustrating, 19
Standards for the English Language Arts, xi
Standards for the English Language Arts. *See*
    English language arts standards
Story elements activities, 77–123
Story webs
    for *Teeny Tiny Teacher,* 21–22
Strega Nona Takes a Vacation activities, 66–68
    language arts standards, 66
    pattern, 68
    skills, 66
Sturges, Philemon, 100–102
Summary charts, 85, 92

Taback, Simms, 9–12
Teacher from the Black Lagoon (Thaler), 156
Teeny Tiny Teacher activities, 19–22
    language arts standards, 19
    skills, 19
    story webs, 21–22
Thaler, Mike, 155–157
Timothy Goes to School activities, 73–75
    language arts standards, 73
    skills, 73
    worksheet, 75
'Twas the Night Before Thanksgiving activities,
    107–114
    language arts standards, 107
    patterns, 108, 109–114
    skills, 107

Understanding the human experience, xi, 23, 26,
    86, 100

Van Laan, Nancy, 115–116
Very Busy Spider (Carle), 128
Very Hungry Caterpillar activities, 134–136
    language arts standards, 134
    pattern, 136
    skills, 134
    transparency, 131
Very Lonely Firefly (Carle), 128
Very Quiet Cricket (Carle), 128

Welcome Back to Pokewood Public School
    activities, 13–15
    language arts standards, 13
    pattern, 15
    skills, 13
Wells, Rosemary, 73–75
Westcott, Nadine Bernard, 89–95

When Winter Comes activities, 115–116
    language arts standards, 115
    skills, 115
Wood, Audrey, 6–8
    worksheet, 5
Worksheets
    for *Alligator Baby,* 28
    for *Bag I'm Taking to Grandma's,* 65
    for *Bark, George,* 81
    for *Big Al,* 84
    for *Big Green Pocketbook,* 5
    for *Cindy Ellen,* 88
    for David Shannon, 141
    for *D.W. the Picky Eater,* 62
    for Eric Carle, 133
    for *Frog Principal,* 45
    for *If You Take a Mouse to the Movies,* 31
    for *Is Your Mama a Llama?,* 36
    for *Jacket I Wear in the Snow,* 25
    for *Lady with the Alligator Purse,* 93–95
    for Louise Borden, 154
    for *Maxwell's Magic Mix-Up,* 48
    for *Miss Spider's Tea Party,* 105–106
    for *Napping House,* 8
    for *Rainbow Fish,* 72
    for *Timothy Goes to School,* 75

About the Authors

Brenda S. Copeland has been an elementary librarian for the past six years in the Palmyra School District, Palmyra, Pennsylvania. She earned her M.L.S. from Kutztown University and her B.A. in elementary education at the University of Delaware. Brenda is very passionate about motivating kids to read. She enjoys being a guest storyteller in her spare time. Currently she and her family reside in Myerstown, Pennsylvania.

Patricia A. Messner has been an elementary media specialist for the past fourteen years in the Lebanon City School District, Lebanon, Ohio. She earned her master's of education from Miami University, Oxford, Ohio, and her bachelor's in elementary education at Asbury College, Wilmore, Kentucky. Patricia is truly a media specialist; she enjoys sharing computers with students just as much as sharing a good book. She spends time volunteering for Special Olympics and resides in Lebanon, Ohio, with her husband, Bill, daughter, three sons, and two cats, Dollie and Dave.

Brenda and Patricia are sisters and grew up in southwestern Ohio. They have completed this book over the telephone and the Internet.